PROFIT OF THE PLUNGE

by

SIMON CAWKWELL
(AKA EVIL KNIEVIL)

First published 1995

British Library Cataloguing in Publication Data. A catalogue record for this book is available from the British Library.

ISBN 0 948035 17 X

Published by:
Rushmere Wynne Limited
Cavalier House 21 High Street
Leighton Buzzard
Bedfordshire LU7 7DN
Tel: 01525 853726
Fax: 01525 852037

Designed by:
MacWing

Printed by:
HS Printers Limited
Buzzard Works Billington Road
Leighton Buzzard
Bedfordshire LU7 8IN

PROFIT OF THE PLUNGE

by

SIMON CAWKWELL
(AKA EVIL KNIEVIL)

Rushmere Wynne Limited
England.

Sun Money

Evil Evel spreads fear in the City

By DAVID YELLAND Sun City Editor

A WHIZ-KID nicknamed Evel Knievel is terrorising the City, Sun Money can reveal today.

Mystery man Evel, named after the motorbike stuntman because of his death-defying feats in the stock market, is making a **FORTUNE** by sabotaging company share prices.

He manipulates the stock market by planting false rumours with City moneymen and financial journalists which he knows will send a firm's share price plummeting.

Shares scam nets him a fortune

His scam works like this: Devious Evel targets a company and starts dishing the dirt. He secretly sells shares he doesn't even have.

This is called "selling short" and is legal because moneymen don't settle deals for two weeks. When the price has fallen he **BUYS** shares in the victim company, delivers them to his previous buyer, and pockets the difference.

Evel is thought to have sold and bought up to 25,000 Speyhawk shares in May, selling at 140p and buying at 99p. He would have made **£10,250** for doing **NOTHING!**

Damage

Last night one of the City's top dealers attacked Evel's tactics. Brian Tarrel of Barclays de Zoete Wedd said: "This practice is deplorable. It can cause massive damage to companies and we can't do anything to stop it."

Companies which have been hit by Evel, and other rumour-merchants, include:

■ Media firm Carlton Communications. Shares fell a **QUARTER** in March when somebody spread a rumour that boss Michael Green had "fled the country."

■ Property firm Speyhawk. Evel told dealers that chairman Trevor Osborne had personal tax problems, which is untrue.

■ Financial services giant British & Commonwealth. A false rumour that chief executive John Gunn had been arrested hit the shares.

★ *IN AMERICA rumour-mongers regularly "kill off" the president to send shares down. One Wall Street dealer said: "There's a joke round here which goes: "Read my lips—the president is still alive."*

Devious Evel plants rumours that send shares plummeting

***The Sun**, 23rd October 1990: I am told that I could have sued **The Sun** over aspects of this article. But I attribute any defamatory remarks to that paper's dedication to fiction.*

I dedicate this book to
Captain Robert Maxwell MC,
captain of my best worst investment

PREFACE

"He that sells what isn't his'n
Must buy it back or go to prison"

Evil Knievil is the nom de guerre of Simon Cawkwell, a chartered accountant, businessman and stockmarket trader. He lives in Knightsbridge, West London.

He is a short-seller of shares. He sells stock he does not own hoping to buy it back at a lower price thereby making a profit. It is quite legal. Spreading false rumours or circulating malicious stories is against the law. Bear-raiders in the City do this and the authorities have been unable to stop it. Evil Knievil claims never to have broken the law. He was once fined by The Institute of Chartered Accountants for failing to pay his gambling debts. As you read his story which follows, you will find that he is quite open about his history.

The name Evil Knievil (misspelt, of course) arose when he was short-selling shares in Maxwell Communication Corporation. In many ways Simon has come to live the part. He has an extraordinary sense of humour and despite heavy editing, it shows through in the pages that follow.

Short-selling is a fact of stockmarket life. The authorities hate it and the moralists despise it. Logically, it is merely the opposite to what most investors try to achieve. And for every buyer there is a seller. It is also extremely dangerous. **The techniques described in this book are complex**

and should not, under any circumstances, be attempted by anyone without first, fully understanding the system(s) and secondly, having the advice of a stockbroker or financial adviser who is fully qualified and registered with one of the investment regulators.

Evil is, unsurprisingly, rather scathing about regulators. And to an extent he is right. Many serious commentators believe it is impossible to produce a fair market place by regulation alone. Education and knowledge are better weapons.

Private investors can be perplexed by the unexplained movements in share prices, often panicking them into illogical investment decisions.

In future, perhaps they should pause and ask themselves "Is Evil at work?".

ACKNOWLEDGEMENTS

My principal gratitude must be extended to the nervous broker who introduced me to short-selling at the height of the 1970/73 bull market in order to protect his firm's exposure to my long positions. Defamation law forbids me naming him, for he is still alive.

Of course, no such inhibition needs be shown in the dedication to Robert Maxwell. Without him, where would I be today? On the other hand, I am sure that he had no best intentions towards me personally. I therefore turn to those who have actively assisted through encouragement or toleration.

One of these, surely, is my wife. She is placid. This is not through ignorance for she is frequently awakened at 4.00 a.m. as I go to my desk to tussle with the figures. She just reckons that fortune favours the bold and the God-fearing. And, since she cannot do much about influencing the practical application by me of either of those two attitudes, there is not a lot to add. She is generally considered to be philosophical.

I have enjoyed dealing through Ilias Mavroleon at Charles Stanley.

Another, if unintended, source of material has been hypocrisy and reserve in the City of London, frequently accompanied by cowardice and obsequiousness. This means that the truth is often only available to those who are prepared to dig while indifferent to the consequences of either the digging or the truth.

My friend, Anthony Rentoul, is a courteous courtier at Conrad Black's *Daily Telegraph.* Anthony tolerated my many mistakes when, some seven years ago, he asked me to nail a fraudster, Ronald Clempson, whom I supplanted as chairman of a BES company, Winebank PLC, in which Anthony had invested. I learnt a lot from Anthony. And one of the things that he taught me was to try to avoid egregious blunders in English. Any success in that regard that this book may evince is down to him. The errors remain mine.

Another friend, Nigel Johnson-Hill, who is an institutional stockbroker, corrected me on a number of matters of fact and, more importantly, very properly insisted that at several points the meaning of my draft was unclear. Any muddles that remain are my fault.

My colleague, Virginia Darbyshire, who has a considerable capacity to organise papers, turned herself away from a few Lloyds' tax loss relief claims to complete the draft.

SIMON CAWKWELL
London,
September 1995

Contents

Author's Note

This book is intended for both the stockmarket practitioner and the serious investor. It most certainly will not assist the legendary widow or orphan (although, in my time, I have met at least one widow and one orphan who have each been perfectly capable of looking after themselves). I know that my book offers a route to considerable wealth. My first short sale was in 1973 and, in fact, initiated and executed (entirely improperly) without my authority by a stockbroker who was concerned to protect me – and, thus, himself – from the consequences of too many long positions. But a moment's reflection introduced me to a new form of gambling and I was thus quite happy to let the short positions run.

Some are temperamentally better at shorting than others. Arguably, such is my own temperament. But I would go further and add that I am much happier shorting than going long. I am sure that this is a character defect which is unlikely to be corrected much before my deathbed repentance.

It is also true that my small accountancy practice, a quiet haven of sanity of twenty years' standing, has on average never made more than half the cost of maintaining my family. And, whereas I used to rely on the gap being closed by gambling on horses (very successfully from 1978 to 1984 – later overturned by losses) the simple fact is that the only long-term explanation of my solvency lies in cash from the stockmarket. This cash has been made chiefly by short-selling.

As it happens, I reckon that any investor who can make money as a trader on the long tack can make money on the short tack. Short-selling demands more discipline since there is less time for errors to be corrected. But the profits can be sensational and, of course, they occur most readily just when losses are most likely to arise on the long portfolio.

I have tried to give you as much practical guidance as possible, primarily by telling my own stories. Curiously, most of the anecdotes I have included recount successes; and, in fairness to myself, I have had a fair number. But even a mildly critical reader will spot that there are fewer references to failures when, in fact, there have been quite a number. This is because, although I show how to identify a mistake and what to do with it, even at this stage, I do not like to remind myself of a particular example!

I should mention that an infamous New York short-seller/speculator of the early twentieth century, "Sell 'em Ben", died broke. I suppose he grew too confident to retain his judgement or was so laced with cynicism that he destroyed himself. You have been warned.

Bon voyage.

SIMON CAWKWELL
London
September 1995

◆

CHAPTER ONE
A POTTED HISTORY

◆

Definition of short-selling and deciding size of exposure to risk

Short-selling (or going a "bear") is the process of selling stock which one does not own in the expectation of buying it back later at a lower price and thus realising a profit. Because there must always be the possibility that no stock is available when one comes to buy, to close the short-sold position, there must always be the theoretical possibility that one can lose all that one has. Indeed, so awful is such a prospect that some otherwise apparently sensible people claim that one can lose an infinite amount of money. But, however much money is in the world, the total is surely finite. So one can dismiss the "infinite" argument against short-selling as the commentary of the cowardly and ignorant – and one always does well by ignoring that lot.

However, one cannot rule out facing technical conditions which can be extremely expensive to surmount. I am here reminded of the bear "squeeze" which arose in Acorn Computers about ten years ago at a time when that company was experiencing commercial difficulty. Although short-sellers were entirely correct to expect declines of the order of 50%+ from the points at which they sold, there was not that much stock about or to be offered by later sellers. As a result, the market-makers (all of whom were perfectly well aware that Acorn Computers was standing at too high a price) simply declined to offer short-sellers stock to enable them to satisfy their short-sale bargains. This was the making of a classic bear squeeze. Before long, one or two short-sellers lost their nerve (this often happens with a short-seller who has not taken the trouble to work out his strategy but, instead, has idly left his decisions to trade to another) and ran for cover. This drove up the price. And only those who had done their homework (and were thus able to resist any argument to justify the new and much higher price) stood their ground.

If I were asked to remark upon a general rule as to the potential loss on a short position, I would reply that a dogmatic view is not possible. The fact is that a takeover bid can be at a 100%+ premium to the current price particularly if market conditions are about to turn to the bull tack. The fact is that a highly geared company, even if in its last months of life, can advance quite spectacularly in percentage terms if the market senses that a rescue can be dreamt up. On balance, one should reserve for a loss of the order of 100% of the opening sale proceeds on each position and, on this basis, never commit oneself to an exposure in excess of 10% of one's net wealth. One must always judge whether one's personal balance sheet is excessively geared even though short-sale positions tend to do better when general market conditions are generally bearish.

Some short-sellers of the past: speculative positions; rapid downward price movements caused in the unwinding of speculative positions; who benefited?

(i) Vanderbilt and three corners

A complete history of short-selling would have to encompass the development of stockmarket regulation and much else besides. Obviously, there is insufficient room even remotely to permit such a (tedious) recital. Further, it would be incomplete in one sense because, as far as I am aware, there are no detailed records of trading on (for instance) the London stockmarket in Victorian times. And I must presume that there are many exchanges around the world whose history has never been closely recorded. For instance, while we are about it, I would not mind betting that the story of Shanghai, to name but one centre, would interest many. The Shanghai story will also remain untold.

However, in the US, they really are interested in the history of stockmarket speculation. While researching this section in The British Library, I came across the title, *Speculation on the New York Stock Exchange, September 1904 to March 1907.* I asked for this title. But the librarian declined to supply it because he decided that I had failed to specify the dates (I had expressed September 1904 as 9/04). I must therefore suppose that there are many volumes dedicated to this one aspect of stockmarket trading. This suggests to me that Americans take the recording of their financial activities very seriously indeed.

Nowadays, one should not, if a director of a company, short-sell the company's stock when a rights issue is on the way. This is because it would be an insider trade. (Mind you, I saw that very conduct several times in the late 1980s.) However, there were no such inhibitions in New York during the nineteenth century. Indeed, it would have been regarded as foolish not to have taken advantage of such an opportunity. That said, one should not be too sanctimonious about Americans: in 1912, Rufus Isaacs, later the first Marquess of Reading, bought American Marconi stock for himself and his Cabinet colleagues ahead of the publication of a contract between the Government and the English Marconi Company. The contract had been negotiated by himself on behalf of the Government. His brother, Godfrey, was a director of English Marconi. Isaacs still became Lord Chief Justice.

There were then many examples of companies controlled from Wall Street by financiers who sold short their companies' stock and then delivered by the simple expedient of selling a "property" (an industrial concern) to their company in exchange for shares. Strictly speaking, this was not short-selling – because the directors knew they would not be going short by the point when delivery would be compelled. But, technically, until the stock had been issued, they would have been short. This technique of introducing "properties" was a clear opportunity to "water" stock. In nineteenth century markets, there was a lot of "stock watering" – a term derived from the practice of cramming cattle with salt so that the satiation of their resultant thirst pushed up their weight at the point of sale.

Many varieties of derring-do were rampant in nineteenth century New York. But, undoubtedly, Vanderbilt's two Harlem corners and his Hudson corner still provoke some admiration for his forthright manner during their development.

The New York and Harlem Railroad joined Wall Street at the southern end of Manhattan to Harlem in the north. It had restricted trading opportunities since it was licensed by the Common Council of New York, the local authority. In early 1863, it occurred to some members of that Council, who presumably owed some duty of fiduciary care to the electors (rather, as I must suppose, did the Marquess of Reading) that it would be a good idea to go long of Harlem stock, grant a franchise to Harlem, and then sell the stock that they had acquired. I am quite sure that it had never occurred to them that this was or would be an undisclosed profit for which, by today's legal standards, they would be obliged to account to the electorate. Further, today, they would be regarded as having breached the obligation of a servant or agent to avoid a conflict of interest. They simply regarded it as a perquisite of election to the Common Council.

Harlem's stock had been standing at $6 in October 1857, attaining $28 by early January 1863. As one of America's financial and commercial titans, Cornelius Vanderbilt took control in the opening months of 1863. The price rose – to $87 by early May 1863. There were 57,000 shares in issue. These figures give some idea of the true forces behind the subsequent movement. I regret that I do not hold indices for either the New York Stock Exchange (NYSE) or railroad stocks in general to allow for adjustment for relative strength. But it is very probable that Harlem had far outperformed the market by early May 1863 notwithstanding the inflationary conditions caused by the Civil War. Harlem may indeed have seemed overbought. The Common Council members schemed first to acquire Harlem stock and then to sell a franchise to Harlem (both of which they did) to extend its operations for 10% of the turnover generated and a flat annual charge of $25 per railcar – a charge, all told, to the franchisee of approximately $300,000 pa. This figure was rated by the market as highly profitable to Harlem. The scheme had the undisclosed distinction of an intention to repeal the franchise after the Common Council members had short-sold the stock.

The combined effect of the Councilmen's initial long positions and Vanderbilt's further purchases caused Harlem to touch $116.25 by 18 May. At this point, the Councilmen clandestinely liquidated their longs through the market to, as it turned out, Vanderbilt and his associates and proceeded to go short. The price declined to $109 by 1 June and $106 four days later. By 9 June it stood at $97.5 and crashed to $83 the following morning, only to recover to $89 that afternoon. However, by 17 June, it stood at $77. And, on 18 June it was traded down to $69.5, even if jumping to $79 in the afternoon.

The Councilmen then decided to cover their shorts. But, being professional men, they did so after announcing that the franchise to Harlem had been rescinded. After all, it helps to see that stock is to hand when one wishes to buy.

However, the stock only fell to $72 on the announcement of the rescission. This was because Vanderbilt was supporting the price. It was then that the squeeze started and, two days later, Harlem had risen to $94. By 27 June, it had touched $106. It was then that the Councilmen met and rescinded the rescission subject to their being allowed to close their shorts at $94. One contemporary writer remarked that "it may seem anomalous that Harlem should rise 30% on the repeal of the grant and fall on the repeal of the repeal". Many would agree even now.

But there was still a short position and, despite civil unrest in New York quite otherwise occasioned, Harlem showed massive strength throughout July and hit $135 by 4 August and $179 on 24 August. The highest bargain was 500 shares at $180. And that was that. The corner was settled and Vanderbilt let the price drift. By December, Harlem stood at $87.5 – which was probably about where it should have been all along. The approximate decline in value of the company from its high was $5,000,000. This is a helpful sum today. But, then, it was astronomic.

Astonishingly, Vanderbilt, who must have had the coolest of cool heads, a sort of cucumber of the century, was simultaneously handling a quite separate operation in Hudson railroad stock. Its price had declined to $123 by 20 June 1863 as a result of a sustained bear-raid. Vanderbilt instructed his brokers to buy all stock that was to hand. He then pulled the master stroke. He sold his stock and simultaneously bought call options to get it back. This was leaked by Vanderbilt to the short-sellers, who, knowing that such a transaction is very expensive finance in effect, judged that Vanderbilt was short of cash. Accordingly, they sold the stock again through the market to, of course, Vanderbilt, who then exercised his options and called for his stock. The bear-raiders looked round for some. It just was not there and Hudson, on 9 July, hit $180 for cash settlement because Vanderbilt had made it plain that he wanted his stock and would not countenance delay – I presume that any failure to deliver under the then rules of the NYSE would have seen the defaulting short-seller bought-in (q.v.) at market price. This price contrasted with the simultaneous price for delivery of stock two weeks later of $150 (I expect that such quotations were borne in mind by Goldman Sachs when they squeezed the London market in Maxwell Communication Corporation stock some 128 years later.) Vanderbilt then lent stock to the market at 2% per day. Nice business if you can get it. And Vanderbilt got it. Having got it, he forced the bears to close and, that done, the price withered away to $140 a week later. Child's play, really.

In 1864, only a year later, Harlem, which was clearly one of those stocks one never holds (because they are only for buying and selling), re-emerged as a scam vehicle. For, despite the New York Councilmen's experience in 1863, some New York State senators, based in Albany, took up long positions and then spread the belief that legislation to assist Harlem's position would be passed. This took the stock up from the low $100s to $149 by mid-March. The senators and their associates closed their longs, opened their short positions and awaited the Senate's judgement. This was indeed that the legislation sought for Harlem would not be passed. And, by 26 March 1864, Harlem had fallen back to $101.

Vanderbilt watched all this and proceeded to build his corner. In fact, he bought so much Harlem stock that his total holding exceeded Harlem's entire issued capital by 27,000 shares. His control of Harlem meant that he knew that there was no chance of more shares being issued. So from its low of $101, Harlem advanced to $122 by 31 March and, by 18 April, to $195. Incidentally, the 18 April sixty day delivery price was $168 – as clear a backwardation pursuant to a bear squeeze as one could ever use by way of illustration. By mid-July, it touched $285. Vanderbilt had played the same stock twice and won.

En passant, I do not think Vanderbilt can have been a very nice man. For it is recorded that, at the outset of the Hudson squeeze, referred to earlier, he had advised his own son to sell 10,000 Hudson shares at $110 – just so that he could get hold of stock. But his son, judging that his father would or might deceive him, bought rather than sold. This made the son a substantial profit.

It will be seen that today's legislation covering disclosure of holdings, particularly directors' holdings and concert parties would make Vanderbilt's game much harder to copy. Indeed, it is probably impossible. I qualify "impossible" because I reckon that it is wise to assume that anything is possible in a stockmarket.

(ii) The Globe Group crash

It is a cynic's rule of thumb in stockmarkets that the more important sounding the name of a company the more probable it is that the concern is inefficiently or badly run. At the immediate outset of the twentieth century, the London and Globe Finance Corporation, chaired by the Marquess of Dufferin (whose conduct, incidentally, is not the origin of the term "duffer") was generally reckoned to be in a fairly strong position and its subsidiary companies were regarded as promising ventures. One of these, Le Roi No. 2, had been the subject of a "rig" (ie. manipulation) for months. Le Roi No. 2 stood at £23 at the outset of trade for Friday, 28 December 1900. The crash was sudden; quite late that day all credit in connection with the Globe Group of quoted companies was found to have disappeared. London and Globe fell from 14/= to 7/6, Lake View from £13 to £7$^{3}/_{4}$, British America Corporation from 13/3 to 8/=, Le Roi No. 1 from £6$^{1}/_{2}$ to £4$^{1}/_{2}$, Standard Exploration from 7/= to 1/=, Kootenay from £6 to £1, Rossland Great Western from £8 to £2$^{1}/_{4}$, and, finally, Le Roi No. 2, the specially rigged concern, from £23 to £3. No less than thirteen Stock Exchange member firms failed.

The cause of the collapse was that London and Globe was supporting the share prices of its subsidiaries and ventures with loans that were called in because the bankers in question judged that the commercial justification for the group and its operations could not be discerned. Thus London and Globe was unable to pay for shares acquired as part of its rigging process. It therefore owed money to jobbers who, in turn, owed money to brokers for short-sellers among others. As a result, London Stock Exchange (LSE) members were debtors to short-sellers, who had sold stock. A "special settlements" committee (which was, no doubt, briefed on the point that many of the various bargains under review did not relate to real concerns and that the participants knew it – such that many of the bargains could have been voided) fixed prices to clear positions. This was surely wise given that a challenge of the bona fides of the short-sellers and subsequent failure to settle them would have led investors to wonder whether a fair deal would necessarily be achieved in future at the LSE.

There is obviously something about the name *London and.....* because in the 1973/74 bear market, the first to go was another share-financing concern, London and County. To my certain personal knowledge, the short-sellers made tidy sums on that one – after all, I made some myself! I do not wish to be thought frivolously apocalyptic. But today's listings on the London Stock Exchange include a fair sprinkling of *London and...... 's*. It is time to get out your notebook.

The settlement of the bargains attending the London and Globe collapse illustrate an important point: stock exchanges have survival as their principal purpose. Therefore, if a member firm gets into difficulties, it is necessary to change the rules if they can be changed and particularly if they can be beneficially (for members) changed retrospectively (as is also considered further on in the section on Wall Street, 1919 – 1932). This is easier than it sounds because the sanction for the aggrieved investor is to challenge the change in the courts. And very few investors are prepared to do that. It took the loss of staggering sums and years of reluctance on the part of Lloyd's investors before it was socially acceptable to challenge that institution's conduct. Elderly stock exchanges attract and achieve the same inertia. They do this through spurious publicity campaigns. One such is that the role of the exchange and its members is to raise capital for industry. But the truth is that the members enjoy making money on the exchange (why not?) and the capital is raised incidentally. It is just that the latter much more truthful description of motive is less appealing should the exchange seek to appeal to the public's better nature.

(There are different ways of tackling this misrepresentation. In 1980, I foolishly bought shares in Mooloya Investments through a broker who was unloading them on behalf of another client. He owed me a duty of care. I acquired them on a "put through" – that is to say, from another client of my broker – and thus outside the market. Mooloya was suspended and, in effect, declared insolvent a few days later and I challenged the bargain. I confidentially asked the LSE investigating committee to consider matters. Within a week of my putting the request, it was clear that the confidence had been broken. The committee advised that the stock had been "bought in the market" and that the bargain could not be put aside. This advice appeared in a letter signed by a Mr I.Yapp. It was too good an opportunity. I left a message for him to telephone his parents on 622 3626. This is the number of Battersea Dogs Home).

(iii) Clarence Hatry

When a short-seller is assessing the mood of the market in general while preparing for the big raids, he is obliged to consider the market's participants who are most prominent at the time. Clarence Hatry started his public financial career in the early 1920s. By 1929, aged not quite 40, he had developed a powerful following from the public, which was indifferent to the wisdom of the ventures proposed and assembled by him. It simply felt that his companies were part of the high speed development of the economy that fortune had dictated as wise and sustainable. Hatry covered all manner of industries: finance companies for stores, automatic vending machines, automatic photography machines and, last but far from least, the rationalisation of the entire iron and steel industry. It is interesting to note that, in principle, if not in execution, these were all sound ideas. But it remains unlikely that any one man could simultaneously co-ordinate the management required to make them succeed.

Hatry's Corporation and General Securities Limited (another example of a name that sounded too important to be taken seriously) had set out in 1925 to arrange municipal loans. It had succeeded. By 1928, Corporation and General Securities Limited's projects were greatly expanded. This required yet more money. But there was only so much appetite for these issues and, as a result, he had to use inter-connected companies and false accounting to make them palatable. There was at least one resignation (by a director who was also a partner in Foster and Braithwaite, the company's brokers – who also resigned at the same time. This was probably an important resignation – Foster and Braithwaite still trade today). This should have warned the market. It failed to do so because, as an authoritative contemporary record shows, it was accompanied by "plausible reasons". The truth is that when the market wishes to be deceived it is quite unnecessary to take any trouble over the matter. The market has already taken all the trouble that is required to deceive itself.

By early 1929, Hatry was desperately short of cash. His municipal loan business was increasingly questioned and he turned to forging stock certificates to offer as collateral. With the money thus raised he forced up Corporation and General Securities Limited's share price and that of each of his other vehicles. The support operation entailed the connivance of a jobber, perhaps sixty brokers on the buying side and a tenth of that number on the selling side. These circumstances must have been noted in the market by short-sellers because brokers tend to be garrulous. And, whereas one or two might be relied upon to be discreet, there is no chance that sixty could be. Short-sellers must have made a fortune.

The bubble burst in September 1929 – the prices of all of Hatry's quoted vehicles halved and more in a day. Dramatically, Hatry asked his chairman, Lord Winchester (who seems to have omitted to take along his rifle), to Room 80 of the Charing Cross Hotel. Hatry, for himself and three associates, said: "We have sent for you to tell you that we are all criminals". After that, they gave themselves up. No defence solicitor today would countenance such frankness. Equally, no alleged criminal would then have had to face the panoply of absurd laws that we have today. Perhaps the moral climate is unchanged.

It has been absurdly argued that Hatry caused the October 1929 crash on Wall Street. The truth is that stocks were grossly overblown worldwide.

To be sure, Hatry had taken advantage of the general climate of self-deception. But the causes of the self-deception were within the hearts of men everywhere and they have been developing since prehistoric times.

(iv) Wall Street, 1919 to 1932 – Allan Ryan

As considered elsewhere in this book, securities industry regulation has been prompted by excesses leading to damage of the small investor or loss of reputation of the market. The reforms of the handling of capital in America (principally those provided by the Securities and Exchange Commission or SEC) were prompted by the period from 1919 on through the 1920s to Wall Street's nadir in 1932. There were many remarkable series of dealings.

The first bizarre series that remains popularly recorded was Allan Ryan's squeeze on Stutz, the maker of the Stutz "Bearcat". By early 1920, Stutz itself was considerably reduced but Ryan, who controlled it and was himself a member of the NYSE, squeezed the stock up from $100 to, eventually, $750. The "Business Conduct Committee" of the NYSE charged Ryan with unethical dealing. Apparently, a number of members of the committee were short themselves. So the committee threatened suspension of the stock from trading – this would make buying to close undelivered short positions according to the exchange's rules much harder. This did not interest Ryan who, although heavily in debt, advised the committee that he would proceed against the exchange to enforce delivery of stock. That caused the NYSE's "Law Committee" to rule that all his purchase bargains were void and that stock would not require to be delivered. The really important point to make here is that if ever one puts market professionals under serious pressure, they will always consider changing the rules to suit themselves. That remains as true today as it was in 1920.

Ryan negotiated and supplied stock at $550 per share to short-sellers. Matters were settled. That said, by mid-1922, Ryan was bankrupt with liabilities exceeding assets to the extent of $32m.

Wall Street, 1919 to 1932 – Clarence Saunders and Piggly Wiggly

Clarence Saunders's Piggly Wiggly was a successful retailing chain of self-service stores which was bear-raided in mid-1922. The stock was $50. There were 200,000 shares in issue. By early 1923, Saunders had pushed the price up to $70. He was well aware that he would eventually have to reduce his personal indebtedness and that this would entail reducing his holding in Piggly Wiggly. So he offered stock through newspaper advertisements at $55 with the difference that he offered them on deferred terms, which meant that stock would not be released by him and thus made available to short-sellers until the final instalment had been paid – this was due nine months after the first $25 payment. Of course, he still possessed about 190,000 shares.

The squeeze started and, by late March 1923, took the price up to $120. The NYSE suspended trading in Piggly Wiggly and, worse, extended the delivery date for short-sellers. This was most unfair to Saunders. Some settlements were achieved with the market at $100. But, as with Stutz, Piggly Wiggly was an unsound company and however much Saunders attempted to manipulate the price the underlying trading position meant any long position was inherently dangerous. Saunders was personally bankrupted in late 1923. Saunders reappeared as "The Clarence Saunders, Sole Owner of My Own Name, Stores Inc." This failed in 1930 because of the Great Depression. He died in 1953.

Wall Street, 1919 to 1932 – Joseph Kennedy

During the 1920s, apart from bringing up a future president of the US, Joseph Kennedy assembled a substantial fortune in films and real estate. He protected it by a timely liquidation before the 1929 crash. But he enlarged it by short-selling. If anyone objects to the influence of the Kennedy family on twentieth century America, he has only to blame short-selling which made the Kennedy family a great deal of money. And money is essential in American politics.

This, then, is a brief record of past short-selling operations. I will now explain how I did it and how you can.

* * *

CHAPTER TWO

SHORT-SELLING (1)

Psychological considerations

Short-selling is usually (but not as its name suggests) a short-term operation. It is possible, as is considered elsewhere in this book, to borrow stock and remain short for many months – perhaps even years. But the generality of dealing is short-term with constant reviews of short-term decisions. This process, even if intellectually rigorously conducted, attracts gamblers. So a short warning is included. It has to be short because this is a book about short-selling and not psychology, an interesting but entirely different subject.

Some emerge as gamblers from childhood and others do not. I did. But my brother did not. And my sister does not even find the subject interesting. So, simply at my personal family level, I hesitate to be dogmatic as to the cause of the gambling streak. That said, it has been argued in *Encyclopaedia Britannica* (and who am I to argue with such a source?) that gamblers frequently experienced or think that they experienced absolute authority in childhood. I think that this probably fits my own position. And I mention this to force the reader to categorise his or her own position. Failure to do so must cause the gambler to fail because he cannot best judge his position if he is unable to understand his own mental disposition. Failure to understand will always cause losses.

So important is this central control that I urge an investor, if he is in doubt, to take professional advice. A moment's reflection will confirm that £250 spent in Harley Street is rather cheaper than going bust. Besides, going bust is inconvenient.

It might be concluded from the foregoing that I would counsel a gambler altogether to stay away from the market. And I suppose that, in a sense, that conclusion is reasonable. However, provided the gambler understands his disposition, I think he must also recognise that he has one priceless advantage, viz. the vast majority of investors are so concerned at the slightest loss that they find it impossible to trade successfully in the short-term. They make a market for those with a steelier nerve and thus, quite possibly, a better long-term view. Nervous investors cannot make bold decisions and, as a result, they make nothing or lose. They can only watch their capital tend to match long-term trends and opportunities in the markets. Their brains tend to atrophy. And they bore the pants off me.

Morality of short-selling

It has often been remarked to me that short-selling is somehow "bad form". Such commentators opine that, in life, if one has nothing positive to say, one should say nothing. It is further argued that short-selling is a negative statement in itself and therefore contrary to society's best interests. But all that a short-seller is doing is reflecting upon his perception of the truth. By the time that a company has entered the short list to be sold, the change in its circumstances has either occurred or is about to occur in any event. It can be argued that rescue finance and/or a rescue order might be deterred by a seemingly artificially depressed price. But that seems a most improbable scenario. Besides, God help the over-confident short-seller that meets the buying orders of a broker for the client who reckons the short-seller has made a mistake about the supposedly beleaguered company. I would also add that forever talking up the value of assets (which process notably occurred through the agency of the Conservatives and their leader in the mid-1980s, particularly in relation to houses) is much more dangerous: when such bubbles are punctured, the fallout is socially much more serious. The proper conclusion is that accentuating the negative to excess is just as unwise as accentuating the positive to excess.

Further, if one buys stock in the normal manner, one is invariably encountering a seller. Is this seller to be pilloried for being negative? Let us not forget that all market-makers are frequently short.

It might be thought that because investment institutions do not generally engage in short-selling there is some reason for this policy based on morality rather than profit. But investment institutions must be careful to avoid offending the managements of potential future investments, so short-selling would not be their natural inclination. Further, such institutions are run by fund managers who are almost invariably proscribed from short-selling on their own account. Were institutions to confront the possibility of their fund managers short-selling through their own broker for their own account but ahead of major disposals by their employers, a major temptation to abuse their clients' interests would have to be faced. It can, of course, be argued that managers' own long positions could be handled and thus abused in the same manner. But the temptation thus arising would be much less frequent unless the fund manager's personal portfolio matched his employer's – and, then, if he is honest, he might just as well invest in his employer's fund.

"Normal" stockmarkets

For many years, Barclays de Zoete Wedd (BZW) have produced a table showing how UK equities have risen from 1919 at a compound average growth rate of the order of 12% p.a. Arguably, anybody who sells a UK equity has to have a compelling reason to do so. But just how representative is BZW's table? Had the index started in 1066 there would have been no constituents. Who decides what goes in and when? Had complete failures left the index when they had gone bust rather than when they had dropped below a level which they had to retain to be within the index, would the index figures and conclusions therefrom have been materially different?

Analysis of "unrepresentativeness" in indices is outside the scope of this book. Actually, my doubts that I have so far raised hardly affect any conclusion that UK equities in particular have been worth holding for a very long time. The story is the same all round the quoted world. But all this "money for nothing" begs the question: just how long will it go on?

We have all seen grand theory books and subscription opportunities available in the stockmarket press. Some go as far as supposing waves of human confidence or the lack of it. These waves are revealed to the authors of such books and thus their readers by a number of different means. They invariably rely upon a step into the unknown at some point. If, then, I myself offer a grand theory, I trust I may be forgiven. As you will, I hope, conclude from this book, I am in practice a sceptic – I instinctively distrust a grand theory, particularly one based on a leap of faith. However, I am most impressed that market indices top when the expectation of the return on capital deployed by the underlying constituents is at its highest. It would be surprising if matters were otherwise.

Perhaps more contentiously, I propose that the urge to invest for the future and thus achieve retained reserves can peak even though the political climate may seem to be at its most antipathetic. If one doubts this, one has only to reflect upon the stockmarket peak of late 1968 to early 1969 – nobody would have suggested then or, indeed, suggest now that Harold Wilson's Government was "pro" business. The fact, however, was that people looked worldwide for a boom to come. Even typically incompetently-managed British business could not escape being swept up in that sort of optimism. Similarly, when Mrs Thatcher came to power in 1979, many sensible people thought that the change in British business conduct would be profoundly helpful towards profits – and so it was. But the market did not really move up until the Reagan presidency unleashed a worldwide boom of deregulation which investors and consumers in the quoted world took as a signal of a torrent of profits to come.

The conclusion from all this is that one must judge when people worldwide do not want capital. Strange though it may seem at first, there is a limit to the capital (or deferred consumption) that people seek. Once that point is attained, the return on capital that societies everywhere will release to capital holders or rentiers will sharply diminish. Perhaps some capital will be confiscated. That has happened before.

Assuming that I am correct in this grand theory, it follows that it is very hard to claim to know what is a "normal" market. Sometimes it is up. And sometimes it is down. But it seems reasonable to accept that a market that can go up for seventy plus years can also go down for seventy plus years. Or, if it does not do that, it can go sideways for sustained periods.

Flat markets are much easier for the short-seller to profit from. These conditions mean that there is no natural rise through economic expectation or inflation. Falling markets are even better. A short-seller might own the world at the end of twenty years. Instead of his headquarters being named Trump Tower, it might be known as The Bear's Den. One can never tell.

However, in the UK for many years, one factor, inflation, has militated massively against short-selling. For instance, in 1975 the then Chancellor of the Exchequer, Denis (now Lord) Healey, was advised by the Treasury that the worldwide credit boom that Edward Heath and Anthony Barber had ridden (and played their part in initiating) prior to Labour's 1974 election victory was then contracting so severely that to avoid catastrophic job losses, there would have to be a massive increase in the money supply to generate demand. Whether that was good advice or not, I would not care to say. Certainly, today's markets would not be taken in by such a policy. However, the FT-SE 100 share index predecessor (called the FT 30 – it was much less representative) doubled in the first three months of 1975. If it had not been for the presence of inflation (which peaked at 25% p.a.) and the expectation of it for the foreseeable future, the rise might have been rather less. Those who were short during that period must have regretted it. In fact, one wag, noting that the offer price of a stock was at a 10% discount to a seemingly certain cash offer to be collected within three months, remarked:"Why hold on in this bid target for 10% more cash in three months when you can double your cash in equities generally in the same period?" The point of all this is that inflation constantly works against the short-seller of equities; and inflation has been with us for decades. Given that we may be entering a period of price stability, it may be that a major factor to consider prior to short-selling points permanently in the short-seller's favour.

Deflation is usually used by politicians to describe a time of declining inflation. It actually means a time of declining prices. As far as I am aware, best current advice to HM Treasury has been that deflation, as politicians seem not to understand it, would entail a massive contraction in demand and thus job losses – after all, why spend your money if it promises to give you more through the simple expedient of sitting on it? That said, deflation may yet come back. If it does, it will do so unseen. Further, it gives the short-seller yet another opportunity.

Finally, although I hesitate to make a worldwide judgement – and such a judgement is essential if any value is to be drawn from this section – I doubt whether the current accretion of profit to holders of UK equities is likely much longer to prove socially tolerable in the UK. If I am right, the climate of inhibition of UK profits is set for a long stay. If it were matched by a worldwide revulsion, then there might be a downwards trend in equities for two or more decades such that "normality" (which is where we came in) might indeed be seen as constant selling of what equities investors may hold. This would be a short-seller's paradise.

Short-selling in North America

All stockmarket operations in North America are highly regulated, in theory. Even so, a considerable number of fraudulent promotions emerge every year (which makes me wonder why expenses are incurred by the market-regulation authorities to inhibit them). Of course, there are degrees. The New York Stock Exchange is based on major companies where proper conduct is generally the order of the day. But, by the time you pass on and up to Vancouver, you enter a fairyland of unashamed spoofery. There, deceit is a brazen art form. So much so (I and a few friends blew £250,000 there in 1989) that I dropped a note to the Canadian High Commissioner congratulating him on his country's good fortune through the seemingly perpetual boost to its invisible exports originating from fraudulent promotions. There was no reply.

In the same vein, I recall that a few years ago a disgruntled investor shot dead a fraudulent promoter in the lobby of a Toronto hotel. I expect both parties felt strongly about the matter. Certainly, such an approach constitutes effective regulation to my way of thinking.

It is sobering to reflect that, prior to 1979, investing abroad entailed going through the dollar "premium" pool because exchange control forbade one's buying investment currency at the rate applying to settlement of an international trade. This curious nannying of the citizenry was abolished by Mrs Thatcher – and quite rightly too in my opinion. The boost to Vancouver sometimes makes me wonder.

Short-selling in North America is as regulated as the other aspects of its markets. The differences from the UK are manifold. For instance, you may only sell short on the "up-tick" – ie. when the last bargain was at a higher price than that which preceded it. You must put up cash or near cash as collateral. And you will undergo disclosure requirements on short positions. That said, the process is much more ordered and organised than in the UK. You borrow stock and bank interest on funds thereby released from the market. A short position can be run for well over a year. On balance, it seems to me to be a much more mature approach – one that stems from a fundamental absence of any ethical objection to short-selling.

CASE STUDY:
Access Satellite

Access Satellite was the first bear-raid that I ever developed in any organised sense. It arose because, in early 1986, I was asked by a client of my office as to the feasibility of buying operating assets of Access Satellite. This company was developed from a shell company, Morland Securities, which had itself originally been known as Malaysian Tin Mining Company. It specialised in a mobile "work platform" which enabled its users to reduce or eliminate the use of scaffolding. Seemingly, the cost of the platform could be rapidly recovered through saving the capital tied up in conventional scaffolding and, of course, the heavy labour costs incurred through putting such scaffolding up and taking it down. Although I understand that this platform is currently achieving some acceptance, particularly in North America, by 1986 it was only marginally appealing. In fact I understand that SGB, the well known scaffolding company, had turned it down before its design was ever taken up by Access Satellite. I do not know why. But, at the time, it seemed strange to me that a potential major beneficiary from this product which also had the expertise to evaluate it should not have adopted it.

However, I had noted the flotation of Access Satellite a few years previously and the adverse press criticism which accompanied it and which had advised that the trading record was altogether too short to allow a proper judgement. But I had then decided that it was far too premature to take any steps on the short tack. Besides, at that stage of its life, the promoter had yet to sell his shares and it seemed very likely to me that Montagu Loebl Stanley, the company's brokers, would take a positive stance towards the company.

It was sheer coincidence that my client approached me about Access Satellite. And, as it happens, it was clear to me that there was no business to be done by me with Access Satellite on behalf of my client. So I asked him whether I was free to short-sell the stock (arguing that I would not have thought of doing so without his having raised the possibility). In fact, I offered him the first sale and thus the first bite of the cherry – he declined, preferring some other fruit, no doubt. There were about 15 million shares in issue and the stock had declined from its high of £3+ to, then, about £1.20.

The market size was in about 15,000 shares on a 2p spread, which was acceptable in terms of dealing cost limits. I sold 15,000 shares. It was then that I had an attack of doubt and stayed my hand.

This was foolish because the best time to sell is at the outset of a move – not when the stock has moved to confirm one's judgement. Anyway, the price slipped about 5p and by then I had had an opportunity to study the accounts. Although the company, audited by KPMG Peat Marwick (no less), was making money, it was consuming cash since the profits were tied up in debtors. It occurred to me that the debtors were not settling their accounts because they might have had some difficulty in satisfying themselves that the goods were of merchantable quality. Further, it had been pointed out to me that there were one or two very large debtors whose failure to settle at all could prove seriously embarrassing. Not merely would the profit record disappear but an insolvent position would probably emerge.

I also bore in mind that this company might have a degree of "pig and pork" in attendance to explain the high level of debtors. "Pig and pork", incidentally, is the process whereby Pig Limited buys from Pork Limited apparently at arm's length when in fact there is undisclosed common ownership of both companies. The result is that profits emerge in Pork Limited such that Pork Limited's bankers are conned into financing, in effect, both companies. The auditors cannot systematically pick it up. And the only financial cure for both companies is that Pig Limited ultimately disposes of that which it has purchased at a profit after covering the warehousing costs incurred. Needless to add, this cure is not usually to hand in time. The practice is fraudulent.

I was then advised that my client, quite separately from his original deal, would sue Access Satellite. This was really all I needed to talk quite confidently to those who would listen. As a result, the shares started to ease down a little faster. I contacted Barbara Conway, who had a column in the *Daily Telegraph*, called "Scrutineer". (Sadly, she died prematurely of cancer a few years ago. She was gutsy and had a clear head.) I drew her attention to features of the company and she published. This made the shares even soggier. I even offered her a ticket to Boston, Massachusetts to attend the submission of evidence in open court: she declined – she already had enough to publish.

By now I had attracted the attention of Access Satellite's management who had understandably identified me as a nuisance. They and their brokers issued a reassuring statement and, for a day or two, it became rather squeezy. You may well imagine that if one has sold 100,000 shares in lots of 5,000 or so at a time because the bid has been so weak, the process of reacquiring these shares can be just as protracted and very expensive as the price climbs away from one.

In fact, I later learnt that the directors had purchased 500,000 shares (about 3% of the issued equity) simply to keep the price up in the face of stale bulls departing the scene and, also, the short-sellers who had got stuck in. It made no difference, the share price just would not recover its verve.

I then hit on the brainwave of approaching one of the partners of the Access Satellite managing director's brokers. I asked him to ask his client whether he would grant me a traditional put option at a cost of 25p to sell 200,000 Access Satellite shares at 90p within the normal three months. In effect, the managing director would have an opportunity to buy 200,000 Access Satellite shares at 65p. His broker asked me for forty-eight hours to think about it. You may therefore imagine my surprise when a few hours later and long before the forty-eight hours' time limit had expired a chap who I guessed was the director in question and a colleague (whom I took to be a potential witness in any defamation action that might be conceived) breezed unannounced into my office in Jermyn Street, London with a request to see me alone. I consented. They demanded to know for whom I was acting. I declined to tell them. I then asked them who they were. They declined to tell me. I asked whether I could take a photograph of them with my Polaroid (I said this was kept in my secretary's drawer – I did not say that the drawer in question was at her home – for the best effect would thus have been lost.) They declined. We then agreed that there was no more to say.

Of course, they had said everything. One telephone call confirmed that I had been talking to the managing director. No managing director who is entirely sane would have dreamt of behaving that way and then failing to disclose his identity. An hour or two later, his broker telephoned to advise that his client was not interested in granting the put option. From there on, it was open season and suspension followed a few days later.

There is a postscript. It covers a technicality. A friend had sold, at my urging, 2,000 Access Satellite shares through his broker at around £1. Since the shares were suspended, he had asked me to ask around for stock. I found exactly 2,000 shares with Smith Brothers (now Smith New Court) at 12p apiece. I bought them through my (a different) broker. But, after two months, Smith had not delivered stock. It only then transpired that the 2,000 that Smith were due to deliver were the very same that my friend had sold them. No wonder they could not deliver. In effect, the matter was sorted out by Smith sending my friend a cheque for 2,000 times 88p. But it is a good illustration of the general point that in the stockmarket you need to keep an open and alert mind.

* * *

◆

CHAPTER THREE

SHORT-SELLING (2)

◆

Development of trading strategy

I have no strong views on strategy. It is not possible to confine oneself to short-selling when a bear market is certainly to hand. One must merely await the moment and never overplay one's hand. This is much harder than it seems.

Timing of opening short positions in general

While it is important only to short-sell a stock that is clearly materially overvalued and which will be seen as such by the market after you, yet within the time required, there is no alternative to weak market conditions for optimum success. I have heard it said that one makes more money in a bear market than in a bull market. One reason I suppose is that exposure to the market can be roughly three times one's long position – depending upon one's collateral requirements. It therefore follows that a 20% decline in share prices in general will yield rather more to you as an investor than a 20% rise. But the reason is more complicated than that. For, although a continuing and well-entrenched bear market will take leaders down by 25% or more, it usually occurs at a time of contracting credit and economic confidence. In such circumstances, the number of companies that can move on to the short list to be sold increases rapidly. The chances of an insolvency rise rapidly. Bankers lose their nerve. Investors readily despair and decline rights issues that would be quite feasible in normal market conditions. Finally, most investors will not short-sell and, like mesmerised rabbits in front of headlights, will not even sell positions that are glaringly overvalued until the brutal truth emerges. The scenario is a killing field for the bold, decisive and level-headed. The trouble is that it is such fun that one tends to forget that a settled time (the usual condition) can return unseen and be costly to cover. The conclusion is simple: if the market really breaks down, instantly accelerate your sales. And the moment it stabilises, cut your short losses in general and be extremely selective about running any short position. Arguably, you should not have more than three serious short positions open at any time because you otherwise run the risk of your concentration and sense of relationship to the positions wandering.

Significance of time in a short position

The argument that time in a short position is unimportant, and that all that matters is the quality of the decision to sell a stock, can be readily rebutted by reducing the proposition to absurdity. For, if time never matters, one has only to sell and immediately buy back. This would be nice for the broker, the market-maker and, of course, HM Government and its stamp duty revenues. But it will not be nice for you. Clearly, time must be allowed to affect the market.

Perhaps your sale has been struck ahead of the weekend's press. Perhaps you have decided that in the event of there being no developments by the following Monday, the position will be closed without further review of the relevant factors. But, normally, you will recognise that the more time that you have the more the price should move your way. Arguably, the only person who might be generally reluctant to keep a position open would be somebody who has misled the market and, fearful of being penalised through sustained buying appearing, banks his turn and departs.

Assuming that you do not think that prices generally or your target's sector will advance, you will seek to buy as much time for your brokerage expended as possible. And, in the UK, that time finishes with buying-in (see *Chapter Four*). This is the moment when the administration system formally advises that, whereas it may wish you well, it is simply not interested in having the wheels of commerce clogged by your uncompleted bargain. Buying-in may be deferred by selling for delivery at a later date. This can be up to 25 business days from the trade or T date whereas 5 business days is currently normal. At the time of writing, it is not clear whether disclosing oneself as short through deploying the T + 25 option in this manner justifies purchasing the extra 20 days. A better trade may be to sell T + 23. Here one's dealer asks for a two way price on T + 23. This raises the possibility in the mind of the market-maker that one is closing a short-sale from two dealing days previously – he may therefore bid you better and not note you as necessarily short. In theory, a market-maker should pay one more for the privilege of paying out 20 days later. In practice, he will not.

As I consider in the section on stamp duty, there is a way round this problem for some sophisticated funds. But it is not generally available to the private investor. He is therefore referred to the section on buying-in.

Stock selection and timing of sales

I am not sure why a short-seller is referred to as an investor. After all, he does not own the stock. He is really a disinvestor. But, and by extension, to refer to short-sale stock selection as stock deselection suggests a process whereby one ceases to be interested in a stock – when quite the reverse is required! Arguably, a stock disinvestor should really also be a very small (one share, actually) investor in the same stock – this is the only means of ensuring that one receives copies of annual reports and notices of meetings. Thus, and strictly speaking, one should be simultaneously a stock selector and deselector. Strange but true.

Enough of semantics! The problem is to find the stock to short-sell. And the only way of which I am aware is to be an avid follower of fashion. This does not mean adopting flared trousers either pre- or post-1970. It means watching the market go barmy with excess on the up tack. This can go on for very long periods. Quite obviously Asil Nadir and his Polly Peck International were riding for a fall if the conduct of his close associates ten years prior to PPI's eventual collapse in 1990 was any guide. But ten years is a very long period in which to stay short. It would be far too costly in dealing and handling expenses even to contemplate. So all that one can do is to note a stock as eligible for a short-sale. One should keep a list and maintain files on all such stocks.

I wish I could pass on the sure means of identifying the moment (in advance of its occurrence) when the fashion fades, but published or prospective press comment is invaluable. If you reckon that a story is seriously damaging to the profit/cash flow prospects of a company, you must also make the judgement as to whether others will share your view, either immediately as you place your order or in due course. If immediately, will they sell at the same time as you (in which case, you may yet have to "pull" or cancel the order on the grounds that their short-term selling will have occurred by the time your order is completed) or will they sell after you in due course so ensuring a superfluity of stock in market-makers' hands to enable you to buy back your position? And will they sell so long after you that superfluity of stock is achieved only after you are compelled by logic or market practice to close your position? You must decide very quickly and on the balance of the probabilities. This is not for those who hesitate or have poor judgement.

Technically, selling a week or two before the publication of results is a sound approach – provided one is reasonably confident that the results and accompanying statement will serve one's purpose. This is not as easy as it sounds. Long before the insider trading legislation ever came on to the statute book, I assisted in the establishment and recruitment of staff for a new company. An obvious opportunity was for me to sell shares in the quoted company from which the staff were largely derived. In fact, the interim results, which came shortly after my sale, made no allusion to the departures which were nonetheless common knowledge in the trade.

It took a further nine months before the full year results formally declared the commercial disaster. It was then that the shares halved. However, some eight months previously, I had to close my short position at a loss of the order of 10% – stamp duty was then 2% which made a loss rather more likely. As I recall matters, the only consolation was that the broking firm (now, and not surprisingly, defunct) through whom I sold, took my failure to deliver stock as proof that they had lost the certificate and, anxious to maintain their reputation, sent me a cheque for sale proceeds as if I had so delivered. Not even a telephone call from myself to advise their error had any effect.

Again, selling in advance of press comment is very attractive provided one reckons that one knows what the journalist in question thinks. This is also not as easy as it sounds. Contrary to the opinion held by some, journalists do not give away the content of forthcoming articles. For theirs is a tough life and indiscretion loses a scoop or, at any rate, a claim to originality. Further, as Hilaire Belloc so sensibly remarked, you cannot bribe or twist the British journalist. You can certainly give him a free lunch. But, as anyone who has tried it will confirm, to demand of a journalist that a free lunch compels a puff in favour of the luncheon host invites a swift riposte. So, and on balance, there is only one way to win the confidence of a journalist and that is to do his work for him. You must find the facts that are new and not understood by the market and, in my opinion, it helps enormously to draft the essential sentences of the article. This skill comes about with time, experience and hard work. I offer no short cut to success here. You must be quite certain that bad advice or, worse, untrue advice to a journalist will cause one to be struck from his presence and that of his colleagues.

Although there are clauses in the Financial Services Act 1986 that strike me as bordering upon the insane (and we should be clear that the Blue Arrow fraud trial, based on the FSA 1986, convicted subsequently-acquitted people and deeply damaged their careers without a brass farthing being paid by HM Government in compensation) there are curious side advantages undreamt of by those who drafted the legislation. I am thinking here of those sections which seek to inhibit market manipulation. They are draconian and, in practice, only capable of quixotic application. The result is that capable research analysts at stockbroking firms are increasingly reluctant to be quoted in the press or even to run the risk of being thought to have briefed the press for fear of encountering a regulator on the rampage. As a result, it is the case that, from time to time, their only channel of communication is through a person whose career and livelihood cannot be ruined by a regulator. This can be you. However, I cannot offer any advice as to a gracious process whereby one can ingratiate oneself with such informants. Further, there is the serious risk that the source may misadvise you. After all, he may not owe you a duty of care. You will just have to take matters step by step. Persistence will pay off. Good manners and humour eventually open almost all the world's doors.

CASE STUDY:
EuroDisney

Timing of short-selling is greatly facilitated by insider trading in the sense of knowing what the market does not, and when that knowledge will be made public. It is doubly assisted by weak market conditions. I now illustrate from an occasion when my assessment was faultless but the truth did not emerge in time.

When EuroDisney was floated by S.G. Warburg in 1989, few can have foreseen the disastrous basics of the business save, possibly, the vendors of the site just north of Paris. They would have known that mud there is the norm. I can only suppose that S.G. Warburg advised Disney in America that it could raise from the public the requisite £1,000m or so cash in respect of 50% of the venture's capital whereas the balancing 50% would be allotted to Disney in America (the parent company) through the injection of a trifling £100m or so of tangible assets. The gap was bridged by mad markets, shrewd marketing by S.G. Warburg and the British and French publics' affair with Mickey Mouse (the affair continues – in 1989 it merely expressed itself in stockmarket terms). I do not blame Disney for going along with this, particularly given the fact that the subscription agreement entitled them to a high percentage of the sales receipts of the venture before a penny piece fell to be distributed to the shareholders.

But weather's weather. And poor Europeans are not as confident as the citizens of Florida (it helps to be confident in Florida to enable one to cope with the local gunmen). Further, EuroDisney was dearer to enter than Disney in Florida. So, by 1992, the price had eased back from its all time high of around £15 – the flotation price had been about £7.50. It seemed to me a clear opportunity to bash the stock by 50% at least.

So Desmond McKey (the bon viveur, gambler and book-keeper to the dentists and doctors of central London) and I short-sold 125,000 EuroDisney shares at c.£9 (the size in London was 10,000 – while in Paris it was three or four times that – so 125,000 was a bit OTT). A fortnight or so later, we got the stock back for around £7.75 and, in the meantime, Desmond had backed his novice hurdler down from 16/1 to 11/2 favourite at Roscommon and trousered a further £94,000 – less helicopter expenses. (He slightly confused the bookmakers by running another horse of his at even money in the first. This horse had looked to be the day's business and it had failed. He made things a little more difficult by switching the novice hurdler from his usual trainer to an unknown trainer some months previously, registering the ownership in the name of an unfamiliar lady, putting up an amateur jockey and instructing his son, Vincent, who was not yet then well known to Roscommon bookmakers, to place the bets. That is how to do it.)

Anyway, after that, as I think you can understand, Desmond and I had a cheerful Saturday's fishing on the Test. That Sunday, I flew to France to rejoin my family on holiday and warned Desmond to leave the stock well alone for the time being. He would not. He doubled his short position at £7.75 and, as the squeeze developed, I even joined him that way again at £9. We had to pay £11.30 to get the stock back. We lost all the money that had been made originally. And the reason is that we were too greedy, encountered generally recovering markets and, above all, a determined securities house touting for the EuroDisney reconstruction business – where the preamble was to support the stock. To put it mildly, this completed the squeeze scenario. Today, EuroDisney is about £2.00.

Short-selling leaders

It is easy to short-sell FT-SE 100 constituents because there are no problems with marketability. And the two exceptional examples of recent years have been Polly Peck International and Maxwell Communication Corporation. Sadly, I doubt if we will get a couple of presents like those two for many years – those companies were really the product of years of general extension of credit by the investing public and, although memories are short, they are not that short!

At this juncture, I would stress that long-term investment is a form of granting of credit – it is just that the management of the chosen company is given the credit by the investor to look after his funds – the only sanction for the investor is a sale of the shares. The result is that fraudulent conduct within a company can roll up for years or, even, decades. The end result is a much more pronounced fall. The only other point is that all people throughout history have at times and in concert unwittingly extended credit to excess. This phenomenon is known as a "credit boom". It follows that all regulatory measures to inhibit such booms must fail and that any money spent on such measures is money wasted. I would not mind if it were the case that regulators were to pay for themselves and were to remain an optional extra – rather like downmarket after dinner mints. But regulators have cunningly leeched on to investors. That rankles. I would not mind if Governor George were to be paid an extra £1,000 a year to be ready to remind investors to go "steady". But the budget for his salary in such matters as control of interest rates already subsists. So I doubt if it is even necessary to spend the aforementioned £1,000.

I have digressed. In general, one should not short-sell leaders. The reason is that they are heavily researched and generate sufficient brokerage for really able and prompt institutional brokers to get their large clients out. Put another way, one is unlikely to identify the 20%+ overvaluation that one really ought to have on one's side before proceeding to short-sell. Over the years, I have occasionally made money on sustained and renewed FT-SE 100 short-sales (I am thinking of Glaxo in the face of Clinton's opening months in the White House). But it can cost something like 15% in expenses in a year and I think it is arrogant at one level and impractical at another to seek to beat the major fund managers by 15% in one year. The fact remains that at a purely personal level, were it not for Maxwell and Polly Peck, I would have lost money short-selling FT-SE 100 constituents.

CASE STUDY:

Polly Peck International

As it happens I had a rather torrid financial time from October 1987 to mid-1990. My firm's overheads were radically increased through a rent review occurring at the peak of the property boom. Further, billings by my firm were deferred or cancelled through the sharp decline of business confidence. To make matters even worse, one or two of the small limited companies that were the bread and butter of my firm's business went bust as the credit squeeze bit. That meant bad debts for me and permanently lost sales. Although the Government was to continue being dramatically foolish through keeping the UK within the ERM until September 1992, my escape from this folly came about by chance.

In mid-1990, Asil Nadir, Polly Peck's charismatic boss, realised that the game could be up and approached a major US bank for finance (of the order of £1.5 billion) to engineer a "management buy-out". This was still quite fashionable then because the banks still hankered after the vast profits derived through the fees charged for such arrangements even though the credit climate had obviously changed to an altogether quieter affair.

In the event, Nadir's proposed lending bank appointed private detectives to check out Nadir. A friend of mine came to hear of points that this enquiry revealed. And if it had not been so serious it would have been laughable. The further rumour arose that Nadir was "cashing and newing" his Polly Peck stock at the end of each account. Such conduct constitutes borrowing at a staggering rate of interest. And it means that either the borrower is mad (and should be avoided) or that he has run out of money (which raises the question as to why) and may well be engaged in a share support operation both to improve collateral values and/or enhance share marketing possibilities.

I concluded that Nadir was not mad and was therefore behaving in this manner through desperation. As it happened he did announce a management buy-out which temporarily caught the market on the hop. However, the evidence that the funds were in place to support the announcement simply was not there. From then on it was plain sailing. Besides, a friend with good eyesight saw police cars prominently proceeding to Berkeley Square and Polly Peck's HQ. My financial affairs were righted.

With the benefit of hindsight I can only stress that Nadir had a hypnotic effect upon many including a sceptical and intellectually rigorous journalist, Michael Walters of the *Daily Mail.* Now, in my opinion, Michael is one of the best financial journalists in the UK today. He has immense experience and he is no fool. But he was quite persuaded that Nadir was a brilliant businessman. In fairness, Michael has always recommended a share on the basis of a stop-loss policy (explained in *Chapter Four*) and had his readers remembered this policy they would undoubtedly have sold long before the collapse and they would still have made a substantial profit.

* * *

The Conjoint Board of Elders of
the Manchester Congregations of Spanish & Portuguese Jews

From: Maurice Mesrie (Hon. Treasurer)
c/o TONATE TEXTILES LTD.
The Mayfield Centre,
Fairfield Street,
MANCHESTER M1 2TT.

Tel: (061) 274-3435.

15th. July 1992.

Messrs. CAWKWELLS,
38a Abercorn Place,
LONDON NW8 9XP.

Dear Sir,

RE: POLLY PECK INTERNATIONAL PLC.

We have received a circular letter sent by yourselves through Nat West Bank Plc. who are holding in their nominee company on our behalf 11595 Polly Peck shares.

Quite frankly our average purchase price for these shares was £2.54 each and naturally it would be nice to realize this cost price back again.

If it is your intention to purchase Polly Peck shares on behalf of your client Messrs. Lumci Partnership, then we would suggest that you make an offer to us for them and we will consider it.

Yours faithfully,

M. Mesrie
(Hon. Treasurer of Conjoint Board of Elders).

Occasionally, as happened here, one finds when enquiring of a nominee registration seemingly large enough (I was looking for 1,000,000+ Polly Peck International) to meet one's requirements that the nominee company forwards one's letter to all the underlying beneficial holdings. This letter came from a bona fide organisation that must have found the loss on Polly Peck most galling. So much so, that a fresh use of "nice" is devised.

◆

CHAPTER FOUR

SHORT-SELLING (3)

◆

Choosing a broker to short-sell for you

Some have argued that, were one able to deal directly with market-makers, one could reduce brokerage costs. And I certainly think that the intelligence of market-makers is frequently overrated – there is undoubtedly scope to beat them at their own game. But, in practice, unless one is conducting a highly controlled and major long fund for a respected fund management concern (where short-selling is, for reasons considered elsewhere, generally and properly banned) it is not possible to deal directly with the market. One must choose a broker.

But there is another reason why a broker is important. He is the only person between you and the market and he can (or should be able to) detect when a position is being pressed too hard. Further, such detection will probably be at a moment when markets are moving quickly. So the first requirement of a broker is that he should not be capable of losing his temper and/or judgement under pressure. Surprisingly, not all those licensed as registered representatives have that make-up. And the philosophical nature required is not normally developed in a broker under the age of thirty. I reckon that as sound a way as any to judge a broker is to take him to lunch. Copious wine soon causes a coarse or inconsiderate fellow to reveal his true self. I may add that, as a gambler, I have tried brokers whom I originally found wanting on this basic lunchtime review. They have proved useless. The cost thus incurred has been considerable.

By and large, institutional brokers work for the larger securities houses. They do not even think of short-selling excepting in unusual market operations associated with major investment or corporate clients. Thus, although intellectually and emotionally up to speed, they are not available. Your choice must be from a predominantly private client-based firm – since a discount broker, the only other type of broker, will not knowingly short-sell. Your choice must evince good time-keeping and sobriety. I do not care whether the claimant has a head of cast-iron; he cannot deal effectively if he is out of his office and/or trying to accommodate half a bottle of gin. Small mistakes, normally overlooked on the long-term long tack, can easily cost a per cent or two from time to time. Since the long term trend of markets is to go up with inflation, these small mistakes can be overlooked when they arise on the long tack but they are intolerable on the short-term short tack. This means that your choice should be a sandwiches and water man in the main during dealing hours.

If your broker is any good, he will have made some money personally by the time he is north of thirty years old – both as an investor and from commissions. He will therefore be able to open a £100,000 position without referring to the compliance officers on the point of credit risk. The other type of fellow who is virtually stony-broke through incompetence or failure cannot assist. And, incidentally, one should be suspicious of a broker under the age of thirty who has made a lot of money on his own account – it is quite possible that such money was not made honestly or, if it was, it was made in such a hurry that his equanimity may not be taken for granted.

Further, the fact is that, although almost any broker you might consider/approach is not going to be an intellectual of the first order (because, if he were, he would not be sitting behind a screen), you should not therefore decline to judge the fellow's brain. Say what you will, brainpower helps in every walk of life. There are all sorts of practical tests. Can the chap do *The Times* crossword? Does he convincingly refer to recent and civilising artistic performances? Is he an expert on gardening? Does he prefer Burgundy to Champagne? This last one is quite a good test because you can be in his presence at that very moment. And so on.

On the matter of personal qualities, I would run the risk of being megaboring if I were to list my selection of essentials for clearance – because we all have our own tests that have been gathered through harsh and extensive experience. But one overlooks this review at one's peril. For instance, a broker who criticises people behind their back yet who declines to do so to their face is not merely a coward, he certainly will not speak for you when the going gets tough – as it occasionally does.

Commission payable to a broker – and how to handle him

I doubt if any private investor is wise to negotiate commissions down to below 0.3%. Although it is possible, any saving thus achieved only puts a broker's back up. In any event, you will have to achieve substantial volumes to agree such a figure. Most investors will not succeed. Personally, I think 0.4% or £40 minimum is fair with (say) £20 as a flat charge to close within 20 business days. I think this entitles one to faxed announcements as they emerge and the expectation of an enthusiastic and creative relationship with the broker and his desk of immediate associates. Apart from immediate settlement of debits the instant they are due, I think the broker is entitled to be able to speak to you in business hours. There is no substitute for a direct line to your desk. Unless severely controlled, this facility can be intrusive into other aspects of your daily life.

But it is wholly unreasonable to disappear for a three-hour lunch leaving your unfortunate broker unable to proceed during fast moving markets and then to expect the best results from him. Do not forget that he, for his part, has to be on parade since shortly after 8.00 a.m. and cannot knock off until 4.30 p.m. or, frequently, later. It is not best practice to make the fellow nervous. It follows that a holiday of more than two business days, particularly where one may not be reached by telephone, is usually best preceded by the closing down of all positions. This means, of course, that no new positions should be opened for some weeks before one goes on holiday. In turn, this may mean no commission for the broker. But the alternative can be tears. I know a broker who went on holiday leaving his clerk to cope with exceptional 10% daily movements in the FT-SE 100 index. When the broker got back there was a bad debt of £1,500,000 to contemplate. I am tolerably sure that this put a dampener on his recollection of the holiday.

It is also important to tell your broker that you are short-selling before you place a sell order. This means that the bargain is booked into a controlled "bear" account allowing your broker to calculate his position at all times. If you do not advise that you are short-selling, the broker will invariably shortly find out and question your every move thereafter. It follows that your broker must work for a firm that will allow short-sales. By no means all firms do.

Collateral

Collateral is almost always sought by brokers acting for short-sellers. A rule of thumb is that 30% by way of deemed value of the outstanding position as ameliorated by unrealised profits or increased by unrealised losses will be sought. So, if you are short of £100,000 of stock, you must have £30,000 with your broker and stand prepared to put up £1.30 for every pound the position goes against you. Cash as collateral is not essential for some brokers. Stock registered in his nominee will do. If it is marketable stock, it may be accepted as collateral up to 80% of its bid value. If it is less marketable stock or spread over few holdings or merely confined to one holding, then the rules can be tightened. And they will be tightened unilaterally by people who cannot profit if you succeed and who may lose their job if you fail.

The result is that, when the going gets tough, you need not look to the administrators/regulators for assistance. They are indifferent to past commissions achieved on your account. The only cure is to keep a very healthy collateral position to hand. Interestingly, I have never succeeded in arguing that a number of short positions tend to render the aggregate exposure in line with the volatility of the market in general and that a reduced collateral requirement should therefore suffice. Further, I have never successfully argued to a broker (he faces problems from the regulators) that short positions will tend to reduce the risk of losing on one's long positions. Of course, one could not advance such an argument where the short positions had come to exceed the long positions or where the volatility profiles of the shorts materially exceeded that of the longs.

Bargain sizes

It is common sense to recognise that however precise and astute one's judgement may be, dealing costs must always be seen as a percentage. Quite simply, minimum brokerage of (say) £25 to open and £25 to close, in addition to 0.5% stamp duty, can add up on a bargain of the order of £1,000 to about 6%. And if a regulator adds on a compliance fee of a further £7.50 (a compliance fee is a charge for being honest and competent – which I have always thought the brokerage firm should be to start with) on each bargain the percentage rapidly rises to about 7%. To beat the market by 7% in a few weeks takes exceptional skill or luck. And those who rely upon luck alone soon get wiped out. The only cure is to increase the bargain size to the point where the round turn brokerage and stamp duty expenses total together under 3% and preferably 2%.

Of course, I have only hitherto considered expenses that one incurs through a broker. No filing system ever paid for itself. Time, even one's own, is not for free. And although the best means of recovering one's own time and administration costs is more and more good ideas, one should never forget that all costs must be seen in perspective at all times.

The other cost arising from using the market is the market-maker's "turn". I do not know how much this is. In the mad days of mid- to late-1987, one could frequently buy and sell simultaneously at around the same price in quite a number of stocks. In that sense, market-makers made no charge to speak of. Then the October 1987 crash came and margins instantly widened as competition in pricing dropped away through the losses and nervousness of the market-makers. I would love to see the current management accounts of the likes of Smith New Court or Winterflood Securities (two well known market-makers), particularly in respect of that latter firm's position in smaller stocks. I would be very surprised to learn that the profit on turnover in smaller stocks is on average less than 1%. And, given that the Securities and Investments Board thinks that the average profit on turnover in all stocks is 0.75%, I guess that it is probably a lot more, particularly with the smallest and least liquid stocks (I consider a typical example in the next paragraph).

Of course, a fiction of service to the public available at the LSE is that where there is in effect (or as overtly stated) only one market-maker, there is scope to trade on the short tack. This fiction is absurd and inefficient. And, en passant, it is not that attractive on the long tack either. However, and setting aside this declaration of personal displeasure, the moral is clear: you must confine yourself to trading stocks where there are at least two market-makers dealing in your chosen bargain size or more. If you break this rule, market-makers will see you coming and show you no mercy. They are only in the game to profit at your expense.

For instance, in early 1994, I decided that Bullers' condition would demand refinancing and that the terms that could be adopted would wipe out the equity of existing shareholders. The quotation was 1p to 1¼p. Normally, given this spread size, I would decline to trade. However, I was so confident that suspension was imminent and that I could thus avoid the consequences of buying-in, I sold 100,000. It was not a big bargain. But it did seem very sound. In the event the suspension was so delayed such that I had to "renew and cash" (see *Chapter Five*). You might think that the market would have accommodated me on the basis of a competitively derived 3% turn or even less – after all, £30 for doing nothing has its attractions. But, because there were only two market-makers in the stock and because that condition is much more likely to produce a wide spread, I had to renew my position at a charge of 1/4p or £250. Bullers subsequently attracted the attention of Jim Slater and recovered to over 20p. However, it is now back to 2p.

Stop-loss limits

This is not a book about investment in general. But readers will be aware that when buying a share it is as well to decide a percentage of weakness in the share's relative strength that will trigger a disposal without the investor hanging on further to review the fundamentals. This is because one can never know all the fundamentals and, if one's own conclusion from them is seemingly overridden to a significant degree, the real prospect of the sellers being correct and the holders and buyers being wrong emerges. Of course, the converse applies with a short-sale: excess relative strength must entail an instant cutting of loss. (There is usually far too little time on the short tack to allow a review in any event). By this rule of thumb, it is possible to miss out on a coup. But my reckoning is that any profits thus missed are much less in aggregate than any losses avoided.

I cannot advise any certain method to determine the percentage of relative weakness or strength. For a low volatility profile company (and short-sell candidates hardly ever fall into this category) I regard an under-performance of 10% as concerning and 15% as the maximum that should be tolerated. Discipline is all in this game and once a stop-loss limit has been set you are bound to damage your equilibrium if you change the limit. So write down the limit as soon as you open the position. You should bear in mind that I am one of the least dogmatic of people: in advocating the unswerving adoption of dogma, I really must have been convinced somewhere along the line.

As indicated above, another problem which arises on the short tack is that a company that is displaying signs of difficulty will inevitably have a much higher volatility profile. If your target has (say) 1,000% gearing, a small improvement in the market's estimation of the asset disposal/gearing reduction prospects must have a marked effect on the share price. So you will have to insert a rather higher stop-loss limit than 15% – I suppose that a minimum of 20% should apply and, in a really volatile position, 50% might be appropriate. You should remember that you can always re-open the position at a later date if it seems to you that the circumstances justify such a move. In this connection, one should always remember the maxim that the first bite of the cherry is likely to be the juiciest while the second will be less so. And so on.

Buying-in: cause and avoidance

If one fails to deliver stock within five business days of it being sold, the central clearing house of the LSE can first give you notice that it will buy you in and, then, after no delivery, that is exactly what it will do. It makes a charge of £20 for each day of deemed default (nice work if you can get it). But, in practice, the threat of buying-in takes much longer than merely passing the agreed or bargain delivery date. So one has some room – although there is no guarantee of it. In 1990 to 1991, when Goldman Sachs was closely associated with Robert Maxwell, that firm's market-making arm was usually the best bid for stock (for reasons of contract that were only disclosed later) and so received the normal long and short-sales of Maxwell Communication Corporation stock. However, when investors missed account day for settlement by delivery of stock, Goldman Sachs compelled cash purchases to cover delivery of stock – this was frequently at a higher price than the normal offer price (one would normally expect a cash discount when paying cash).

You have been warned – exceptional circumstances can return. Although I have always assumed that the LSE's buying-in office does not disclose the fact of short-sold stock (as indicated by frequent and substantial delays in delivery), the market eventually notes that stock is not being delivered. Occasionally, it puts two and two together. That is also an occasion to avoid. In my experience, the buying-in office do their work fairly and reasonably. But they will buy you in and they will not discuss with you whether they should pay more to do so – this can be suddenly very costly for you. They, on the other hand, are just obeying the rules.

Covering in ADRs

It is sometimes forgotten that, although one might be deterred from taking a strong short position in the UK market because there is only a small "float" of shares, the target company may have issued ADRs (American Depositary Receipts) typically quoted on the NYSE. This means that one can in extremis cover in New York in respect of a UK sale. However, there are a number of drawbacks.

Virtually all American stockbrokers are difficult to deal with unless you trade with them frequently. As a result, if dealing occasionally, one has to treat them carefully and cautiously. This is exhausting if one is accustomed to dealing with one's British broker in a courteous fashion. For instance, one should never deal with an American broker unless one has a clear agreement in advance of dealing as to the commission to be charged. As one well known UK market dealer once told me "the value of goodwill ascribable to an American stockbroking firm is twenty-four hours commission". I suppose he should have added "as reduced by provisions for the cost of litigation arising from the dereliction of employees now departed". Strangely, this will still give a positive value despite litigation being extensively in prospect! But, that hurdle aside, you then face five business days before settlement in US dollars and, then, a delay of about a week when converting the ADRs to UK stock ready for delivery. Typically the cost of this conversion is about 5% and arises because the New York ADR official holder/registrar faces no competition in the UK when asked to effect the conversion. That said, you cannot be backed into a corner simply as a consequence of the UK technical supply position. It helps if you are based in London so that couriers may be deployed and controlled to ensure that no delays occur such that one is bought-in in London before one has had an opportunity to deliver. I have, of course, here set out a reserve tactic if the London market looks particularly squeezy. It stops one having to rely on London market–makers getting round to arbitraging between London and New York.

Handling positions in the light of press/other commentary

Even experienced short-sellers sometimes forget that for every sale they transact there must be a corresponding purchase. And, after the sale, there must be other sellers to follow – the price will most probably not otherwise decline. The consequence of the first point is that the short-seller must be modest enough to realise that he could be misinformed.

It is not therefore wise to keep selling just because the price has gone down or seems to have broken a chart point. The fact is that the bulk of one's selling should be done at the start of a short-term decline. Similarly, if a stock has been lambasted in (say) a week of press comment followed by another dose in the weekend press, the chances of being well advised to sell on the following Monday are very slight because all the short-term selling that can occur has occurred. It is therefore foolish and irrelevant to regard the fundamental case for selling on such a Monday as so strong as to be able to override the fact that selling by others will not occur after you have made the proposed Monday sale. To be sure, after the inevitable "dead cat" bounce/recovery as "bargain hunters" and short-sale closers buy, a fresh opportunity to sell will present itself. This is particularly true if the company comes out with some totally ridiculous statement to reassure investors. You can usually tell when such a statement is ridiculous because the tone is wrong.

The one I like best is the company's advice that "at this level, we are bound to be bid for". No company in history has ever been sensibly offered for sale in this manner. Therefore, such a remark is a declaration of open season. There are hundreds of variations of the informative remarks/ announcements syndrome. You just pick them up as you go along. For instance, an announcement that springs to mind was to the effect that Tiphook's chairman, Rupert Hambro, had bought a mere 5,000 shares at 315p as the price slid away. A chap with the sort of money that Rupert Hambro commands should not be followed unless he lays out in excess of £100,000.

Suspensions: cause and consequence

The origin of suspension of trading of a particular stock (as opposed to suspension of an entire market to achieve orderliness in general) is that the authorities do not want the appeal of stocks in general to be diminished by allowing a "bad apple" to be quoted. It is argued that experience of such a "bad apple" can put an investor off for life. And, quite sensibly, the authorities get their lunches paid out of a central fund topped up by brokers whose income is derived from brokerage which would, in turn, be diminished by the departure of a disillusioned investor.

The initial act of control of a "bad apple" is to avoid it being quoted at the outset. If one were to promote a company to grow bananas on the moon (so as to replenish passing experimental monkeys) one might attract the occasional lunatic to cash in his savings plan to get in on the action, particularly if he were misadvised or insufficiently restrained by a commission-hungry broker. For this reason, all new quotations have to pass muster in principle before trading begins – the "listing" process.

Please rest assured, mad days at the top of bull markets do see some pretty improbable propositions put to investors and getting quoted – these propositions just go down on the list of stocks to sell after a decent interval during which the price is supported by the company's brokers and the founders of the scam are allowed to unload a material amount of stock.

The next stage of the life of a company is that of quotation during which the directors are obliged to request the LSE to suspend trading in their stock if the company enters a critical period (either up or down). This can be temporary, although when insolvency beckons, it is usually terminal. And the question is what happens to the position of the short-seller given that he has no overt market in which to deal to cover?

Now, it is possible to buy to close a suspended stock from a market-maker – provided that he has some. Quite possibly, no stock is available. The only certain cure is to deal directly with other shareholders revealed by the company's registrars. The registrars may not have had their bill paid and, as a result, they simply decline to maintain the register. But a copy is nearly always available made up to a date at or shortly after the terminal suspension. For a small company it will cost about £50 – this process is statutorily capable of being ten days or a little more in practice. For a larger company the cost can head up towards £250 or more. And I imagine that the register for ICI or Glaxo would be a great deal more – it is merely that such companies are not likely to go bust in our lifetimes – although they will do so eventually because all companies, even if taken over, eventually go bust. Ashes to ashes. Dust to dust.

Sometimes, one may imagine that a sufficient block of stock is held in a nominee name. A letter sent by way of enquiry is quite sufficient. The maintainer of the nominee account then forwards a copy of one's letter (assuming that he is so minded) to those beneficial shareholders behind the nominee registration. This can produce some rather sad correspondence from people who are clearly confused and irritated.

Having identified a potential seller from the register you telephone him and agree a price. This is not easy if the luckless fellow adored the chairman of the company or, worse, regarded his investment as a participation in the greater game of life. The fact is that feelings have probably been seriously bruised. And then there is always the hopeless and residual belief that the crook behind the failed company will resuscitate it. You will be amazed to learn that long after Nadir had left the UK for good to avoid trial, I encountered people who still reckoned that he would return to salvage their Polly Peck–based fortunes.

For some weeks after Maxwell's death, I spoke to investors who reckoned that Maxwell had not really drowned and that some deal could be cobbled together to assist them. Other investors whom you identify as potential suppliers of stock will not trust you but, instead, will telephone their broker, who, incidentally, is not generally allowed to act in relation to a suspended stock outside the market because of regulatory controls. He may offer advice, but since he has no commission in prospect as an incentive to complete the deal, no business transpires.

This quite staggering imposition of inefficiency works to the short-seller's advantage because the very people best placed to complete the matter efficiently are denied the opportunity. As a result, the competent short-seller is usually the only person to make an effective enquiry of a hapless shareholder. Thereafter, it is a buyers' market all the way. It is necessary that the vendor of the stock you seek signs a transfer and you will need to have it stamped by the Inland Revenue (0.5% rounded up to the nearest 50p). Their address (you just send the transfer and your cheque) is Bush House, Strand, London WC2. Then you submit the stamped transfer and the certificate to the company's registrar, which, for no charge, will let you have your certificate back within (say) a couple of weeks. You then deliver this to your broker to complete the bargain and await your cheque.

It has been remarked that a suspended but open position presents no risk to the broker and that, therefore, he should not pine for it to be closed. However, and in fact, there is a counterparty risk in that the market-maker to whom the stock was sold could go bust in the interim before delivery of stock is effected and cash paid out. That said, this point strikes me as rather theoretical because my impression is that market-makers are not stupid and are well capable of limiting their exposure at the appropriate moment.

I have taken some time to delineate delays and obstacles. This is because some want their cash immediately – bookmakers' bills, school fees and the like can crop up most inconveniently. But I regard it as bordering on the criminally idle to short-sell stock at £1 and then to buy it back from the market at 10p simply to achieve the certainty and convenience of a closed position when a few weeks' delay and a little patience can yield a further 8p profit. After all, circa 8% extra profit in two months is not bad and it gets even better if you compound it another two months on. Anybody who thinks that this 8% does not assist is probably barmy.

As a rider, and from experience, I can also advise that no banker yet created will lend against the security represented by the yield to come on a short position. Intellectually, banks cannot cope even when the proposition is cast-iron. The reason is that bankers who are capable of understanding and are available at personal customer level are too imaginative to be licensed by the regulators. Such bankers do not therefore exist.

Setting closing bargains against open positions

Quite possibly, a short-seller may increase his short position a few days after the original sale before any question of his being compelled to buy to close the first sale. Then, rather than his awaiting being compelled to buy to close, he elects to do just that. Frequently, he has the option of setting this first closing bargain against the second sale – of course, he might not wish to do so on the grounds that, since he has incurred the expense of opening the second position, he would wish to run it as long as possible. But, and nonetheless, he may prefer to set the closing bargain against the second sale because the profit is greater and he would prefer the cash sooner. It is a small point. But in the short-selling game economy and versatility are essential.

CASE STUDY:
Maxwell Communication Corporation

The Polly Peck profit was in the bag by late September 1990. And, although the credit climate was still puncturing reputation after reputation, it never occurred to me that there could be something bigger and better than Polly Peck. How wrong I was!

For most readers, the Maxwell life story has been recited too often to justify its inclusion here on anything other than on an outline basis. He was born in Czechoslovakia and first entered British consciousness with his rank of captain right at the end of the second world war. He would then have been about 22 years old. He picked up a Military Cross. This established him as brave. But his business career was one confidence trick after another. By 1980, he had ceased to be a Labour MP and was widely mistrusted and disliked. For instance, Sir Sigmund Warburg opined that Maxwell had betrayed his fellow Jews through his misconduct. But Maxwell frequently deployed lawyers to issue gagging writs and, as a result, the truth as to his nature was not generally known.

So, in the early 1980s, he managed to save British Printing Corporation (itself created in the late 1960s by a strikingly ambitious fraudster). Maxwell just bullied the print unions into submission. This outcome was long overdue. No one had hitherto had the guts to do it. It is sobering to reflect that had the unions not been so obstructive they would probably have ended up with a management that would not have stolen their members' pension fund.

As a result of this coup, the banks warmed to Maxwell. And BPC (or Maxwell Communication Corporation as it subsequently became) blathered on through the 1980s. By 1990, the balance sheet was crammed with intangibles – two major purchases in the US had produced that result. Further, Maxwell owed substantial debts secured on his shareholding in MCC, then valued at about £1 billion. But the shares were descending and thus the expected yield based on historic declarations was rising as investors scented a cut in the dividend. By October 1990, the indicated yield was of the order of 15% – or at least twice the general yield on FT-SE 100 stocks.

That said, the announcement of the 31 March 1990 results confirmed the dividend and Maxwell himself announced that he would take shares in lieu of cash as his dividend because he believed so much in the company. He forebore to remark that there was no cash available with which to pay him a dividend and that he had persuaded the bankers to lend against the shares issued to him by way of dividend.

The birth of Evil Knievil

However, the cash actually being generated within MCC was a great deal less than extrapolations of the accounts indicated might be the case and informed investors had started to wonder just how representative of MCC the accounts could be taken to be.

My first sale was at £1.45. It was on 3 October 1990. The shares eased a little. It was then that a friend called at my office. In a brilliant brainstorming session he and I wrote a note about the accounts of Maxwell – it always helps to prepare a note to clarify one's mind. This note (which is reproduced in its entirety at the end of this section) was simply a sober reflection upon truths. I wanted to fax it to all the market-makers in London to make quite certain that they would mark their offers down before I was obliged to close. My friend was not so sure – he was then better acquainted than I was with the provisions of the FSA 1986 and, in particular, S47 (which, incidentally, tends to stop truth emerging).

But I was not deterred and even though he would not sign the note I had to give it an authorship. Judging that it would be a little conceited to suggest that I alone was the author, rather than type my own name, I chose ***Evil Knievil***.

A few days later, a journalist on the *Sunday Times* enquired as to whether any one individual was responsible for the widespread nervousness in the MCC shares market. Of course, the simple answer is that nobody can be – nervousness is just a collective phenomenon. But, just for the hell of it, I remarked that the ringleader was called *Evil Knievil.* It made good copy.

By then, *Evil's* note had been faxed round the City and Maxwell had got hold of a copy. It was immediately branded a dreadful slur – no doubt upon a "great and patriotic Englishman" or some comparable pomposity – why people were ever taken in by his style beats me. If I had to guess, I would suggest that Maxwell always paid very well those who acted directly for him – after all, it was not his money! Quite a number of these people were respectable although, in effect, not extending credit to Maxwell. Further, they had no public duty to make known their personal feelings about their paymaster and, arguably, they had a professional duty not to make any comment at all.

As a result, many others were fooled into thinking that Maxwell himself was respectable. It does not follow in logic. But that is how the human brain often behaves – it tends to judge a man by the company he keeps. At the time, Maxwell had an undisclosed arrangement with Goldman Sachs such that that firm's market-making arm had every incentive to buy yet more shares – at the end of this section on page 86 you will find the print out which was obtained from MCC showing the positions of all the market-makers at around that time – you will note the staggering size of Goldman Sachs' long position. It was way beyond normal trading requirements. Further, as a market-maker one would have to be powerfully persuaded that the stock would rise to justify such a position. To this day, I do not know exactly what persuaded Goldman Sachs. I can, of course, guess. Also at the end of this section on page 89, I include Michael Walters' "Why share dealings matter to Maxwell" from the *Daily Mail* for 11 October 1991.

On 12 October 1990, in London dealing hours, a broker, Peter Marks, of Branston and Gothard, (sometimes jocularly, if quite unaccountably, referred to as "Pickled and Ready") sold stock to Goldman Sachs. He then asked the dealer to telephone him back. The record of that conversation is confused. But it was later alleged that Marks had informed the dealer that "Maxwell would file for bankruptcy in New York that night". Seemingly, Goldman Sachs passed this on to Maxwell who then bullied the London Stock Exchange into making enquiries.

As a result, Marks was charged with a breach of S47 of the FSA 1986 on the grounds that he had spoken recklessly on a matter affecting the market. This was a serious charge because its prime effect could have been the destruction of Marks' career. I did not learn of this charge until January 1991 through a chance remark by a journalist whose principal purpose was to warn me that Maxwell had put two detectives on my trail and that, further, Maxwell had arranged for my telephone lines to be tapped.

I do not know whether Maxwell ever took such a step – he was skilful at deviously disseminating through unwitting contacts the possibility that he might prove a threat – in this case, a colleague of the journalist who informed me may have been the means. I have always worked on the assumption that my telephones are tapped – any tappers hired by Maxwell must have had a thrilling time listening to my daughters booking tennis lessons and so on!

However, I was not to know what was actually happening in Maxwell's affairs. And, what with the Marks charge (which I knew to be defective because it could only be brought on the basis of evidence from Goldman Sachs – you will recall the secret agreement between that firm and Maxwell) and because I was repelled by the obsequious conduct of the LSE towards a proven bully and because of further points that were emerging, I redoubled my efforts to get to the bottom of the Maxwell matter. It was slightly a case of "I'll get you before you get me".

I should remark at this point that I had covered my short position in MCC at a small profit in late October 1990. This was because the price was not easing back. Instead it was showing remarkable resilience. Since I had only just escaped penury through the intervention of Polly Peck, I was in no mind to return to zero. I declined to run the risk. I also bore in mind the rule that, in a sense, the market is always eventually right. What this means in practice is that if the expected does not occur in the market, you must reflect on the possibility that you are wrong.

And, much to my surprise, the price of MCC forged up – eventually to £2.40. We know now that Maxwell, realising that his entire edifice depended on borrowings secured on his MCC stock, was stealing funds from MCC's employees' pension funds at an unprecedented rate so as to fund his purchases of MCC stock. At the time one could only guess the reason for the rise. It seemed wholly unjustified by the probable trading position.

Maxwell always confused his private with his publicly-quoted and shared interests. If you like, it was a clear case of "pig and pork" – see *Access Satellite* on page 40. However, one of his private interests was Mirror Group Newspapers (MGN). And, despite Maxwell's ridiculously erratic management of that business, it generated a lot of cash. Since his bankers had by January 1991 decided that they wanted their personal exposure to him repaid or reduced, he was compelled to float MGN. Needless to add, this was accompanied by the usual preposterous huffing and puffing. And he so forgot himself as to include in the press publicity process to promote the sale the oral advice that the Mirror office buildings would also be sold. The drawbacks to this claim were that it was in public and, perhaps more importantly, the buildings could not possibly be thus sold – they belonged, in effect, to another. Of course, only a desperate businessman is so casual.

The Mirror flotation proceeded. The Americans particularly warmed to the idea – they rather like a chap with chutzpah – and, whatever one thinks of Maxwell, he certainly had that. This was completed by May 1991 and the issue immediately went to a discount. The reason was obvious. The British market sensed that he would steal money from anywhere and that the Mirror Group and its pension funds would do just as nicely as MCC's notwithstanding the "ring-fencing" so carefully included in the prospectus. There had been a number of stories in the UK press concerning MCC's and other Maxwell interests' pensioners, both current and prospective, wondering how their future lives were to be financed.

Then there were whispers that Maxwell had stolen £60m through the acquisition of Tokyo Investment Trust. At the time, the acquisition was hard to explain – after all, what conceivable expertise could Maxwell bring to bear upon Far Eastern investment? But, a moment's reflection showed that the only purpose could be a desperate attempt at wrenching further cash from absolutely anywhere. It was time to reflect upon the fact that MCC's price was easing back from what was to prove its high for 1991 – £2.40.

Although the evidence of forthcoming insolvency was accumulating daily, I kept my mind ever open for more. This particularly arose through Maxwell's purchase in early 1991 of New York's *Daily News*. The owners were so disgruntled by the American print unions that they were prepared to pay Maxwell to take the company off their hands. Needless to add, this was manna from heaven as far as Maxwell was concerned and he motored his yacht *Lady Ghislaine* along the Hudson River. However, even though he may have been preposterous in his general behaviour, not even he could have justified his negotiating in New York while permanently and seriously drunk on brandy – and this was reported to me to be the case. The only conclusion was that Maxwell had finally gone mad. He was no longer remotely in charge of his destiny.

By mid-1991, some 25% of MCC stock was held by small investors for reasons of history. Either they had held BPC in the late 1960s or early 1970s or they had come aboard with Captain Maxwell. Such investors do not readily panic. Certainly, all UK institutional investors had left the party. As a result, it had taken relatively little buying by Maxwell's clandestine off-shore fronts to hold the price up. But, of course, he was desperately short of cash notwithstanding the enhanced borrowings created by the rise in the collateral presented by MCC stock. So sellers outweighed buyers. And, as the price of MCC declined during the late summer and autumn of 1991, the banks which had lent on the security of collateral which was reducing in value could only be satisfied by sales of MCC stock. And the only effect of that had to be to compound the problem.

The last weeks of Maxwell's life have been well documented elsewhere – particularly in Roy Greenslade's* excellent account. So I shall desist from making further points. Except that I will never forget the morning of 5 November 1991 and the breach of the chart point of £1.40 – where, it will be recalled, I had originally sold in October 1990. This was the point where the collateral decline became completely intolerable. As soon as stock was offered at £1.39 I knew that the game was all up and persuaded several friends to sell with aggression – something of the order of 1 million shares. The market took it in lots of 100,000 and the final sale at £1.25 was actually achieved in a lot of 10,000 only – the market was sated. That afternoon, Maxwell's death was announced.

The circumstances surrounding the flotation of MGN are currently the subject of a DTI enquiry. Perhaps it would be wiser to await publication of that report before issuing an all-embracing opinion. However, I am reasonably confident in remarking that it was cowardice by hundreds of potential whistle-blowers that allowed Maxwell to ruin so many. No legislation will ever eliminate cowardice.

Peter Marks used my advice that there was no chance of the Crown's prosecution succeeding. He was, of course, acquitted. I still cannot fathom why the DTI ever brought the prosecution.

**Maxwell's Fall* by Roy Greenslade, Simon and Schuster 1992.

Selected documents from my time on Maxwell (October 1990 to November 1991)

As far as I am aware, my review of the accounts of MCC which is reproduced on pages 82 to 85, (its trading screen abbreviation was MWC – to distinguish it from MCC, the cricket club just round the corner from my then home – whatever Maxwell was, he was not cricket in spirit) for the year ending 31 March 1990 was the first such review that was made publicly available. It was faxed and despatched everywhere rather as the Samizdat press of the former communist countries. But many analysts deployed by the major brokers had come to the same conclusions. Their trouble was that they were inhibited by defamation law and commercial considerations from letting their views be known. Further, I know that one major clearing bank (defamation law precludes my naming the bank and thus identifying its cowardice and obsequiousness) sacked its broking subsidiary's media analyst for daring to speak his mind. Had I been one of its clients I would have slightly wondered what else this broking firm as agent, which owed me a duty of care, was suppressing.

I typed it out myself using, as you can see, a correcter ribbon. The ribbon was hard at work. But it was all worthwhile because Maxwell went incandescent when he read the review. It seemed then and it seems to me now to be pretty mild.

I do not know why *Evil Knievil,* the nom de guerre which was generally taken up by the press, first emerged from my typewriter as Evil Knievil. I can only suppose that, in my mind, he was so evil, he had to be doubly evil. Then again, I do not know all the usages of "evil". For instance, my elder daughter currently advises that an invitation to tea can be "wicked".

The printout of Sepon-registered holdings in MCC shows the position that Goldman Sachs had built up as a consequence of the put option that

Maxwell had granted to them. I do not like Goldman Sachs since, in my opinion, they are not clubbable. It is true that not everybody would regard this as the acid test. But it will do for me and mine.

I have mentioned earlier (see Polly Peck) that I think that Michael Walters is good news. What readers may not know is his astonishing capacity to produce a sound article at short notice, based on all currently considered facts. Whether he deployed this talent on the Maxwell articles now shown, I cannot say. But, from some *Daily Mail* articles that appeared, I have selected: 12 February 1991 "Stirring up Maxwell house", 28 September 1991 "Globe-trotting Maxwell seeks a great escape" and 11 October 1991 "Why share dealings matter to Maxwell". They were good journalism then. They still read well now.

I have excluded a copy of a newspaper article announcing Maxwell's death. It is hardly ever wise to dance on someone's grave.

Review of accounts of Maxwell Communication Corporation PLC ("MWC") for the year ended 31st March 1990, prepared by Evil Knievil

SUMMARY

The reported profit for the year ended 31st March 1990 of £101.1 million is entirely attributable to the accounting treatment of the company's acquisitions and disposals together with non-recurring items.

The maintainable profits, and thus their expectation in future years, are negligible. In effect, therefore, MWC has been paying dividends out of capital. Accordingly, unsecured lenders should be concerned at the level of cash dividend payments.

The disposals of shareholdings in Donohue, Quebecor, De La Rue and the Italian interests will be completed subsequent to the half-year ended 30th September 1990* when US 410 million dollars of debt repayment becomes due. Thus, MWC is likely to maintain the interim dividend and the financial impact of the disposals will not be fully known until the release of the figures for the year ending 31st March 1991 in mid 1991.

*and before 23rd October 1990

The market values of the underlying assets (which are mostly intangible) are probably significantly below book value. Given the very high level of debt, MWC shares offer little, if any, underlying value. If the company were to default on interest or debt repayments and were placed in administration, there would be little prospect of any pay-out for shareholders.

NOTES

1. On consolidation of the acquisitions of Macmillan, OAG and Merrill Publishing during the year ended 31st March 1990, MWC revalued the fixed assets* to 'fair value' to the extent of £163.1 million above the cost of the acquisitions but also made provisions for integration and reorganisation totalling £76.7 million which were taken direct to reserves, i.e. not through the profit and loss account. However, in the same year, MWC utilised provisions of £84.3 million which appear to have been credited through the profit and loss account. On this basis, the reported profit before tax of £172.3 million should be adjusted downwards by as much as £84.3 million. Attention is drawn to the Source and Application of Funds Statement and to Note 29(b) to the Accounts.

*and investments

2. Other operating income of £47.9 million, sales of publishing titles of £18.9 million and non-compete agreements of £6.2 million have been deducted from operating costs. Particularly interesting is 'other operating income' which is up by £40.2 million over the previous year and includes £41.0 million profit on property development and sale of property development companies; these are clearly non-recurring items. In any event, the accounting treatment of deducting these profits from operating costs distorts the analysis of gross margins which the chairman claims have improved as a result of the switch from low margin printing to higher margin publishing.

........2

The original "Evil Knievil" note on Maxwell (continued on pages 83, 84 and 85).

3. Non-recurring net gains on sales of investments less provisions of £18.3 million have been deducted from net interest and investment income. See Note 7 to the Accounts.

4. The accounting treatment of the acquisition and subsequent disposal of Maxwell Graphics illustrates that the financial statements do not, in my opinion, give a true and fair view of the financial position of the group. On acquisition of Maxwell Graphics, MWC wrote off £199.3 million of goodwill direct to reserves, thereby reducing the book value in the consolidated accounts. Subsequently, Maxwell Graphics was sold at a profit of £24.6 million by relation to written down book value and this amount was credited to profit and loss account as an extraordinary item. This item, considered in the Report of the Directors on page 29, is further detailed in Notes 4 and 9 to the Accounts. Note 4 advises that this treatment was in accordance with the Group's accounting policy. The important issues raised by this transaction are (a) the accounting treatment of writing off goodwill in the case of Maxwell Graphics is surely inconsistent with the accounting treatment adopted for the acquisitions of Macmillan, OAG and Merrill Publishing - described in 1. above. (b) the extra-ordinary profit is a major component of the reported profit attributable to shareholders.

5. Since the acquisition of Macmillan, MWC has made several disposals. However, in a number of instances, the businesses have been transferred to partnerships and associates at high book values or MWC has received securities rather than cash. Thus, it is critical to assess the value of the partnerships as well as these securities held by MWC. For example, the sales of investments in the Michie Company, Intertec and Webb Publishing in December 1988 yielded an aggregate consideration of US 305 million dollars in respect of which MWC received deferred loan notes with terms of 10 years and coupons of 8 - 10 % p.a.* Were these loan notes disposed today, MWC might receive US 200 million dollars or less and thus incur a loss of the order of US 100 million dollars.

*See Note 19 to the Accounts.

6. Another issue is the underlying value of the recently formed Macmillan/McGraw-Hill partnership which is in the books at £405.7 million - see Note 15 to the Accounts. The partnership comprises businesses which were transferred at a very high book value based on the following analysis: The partnership contributed sales of £96.4 million and an operating profit of £5.6 million for the period 21st July 1989 to 31st March 1990. Applying an earnings multiple of, say, 13 times post tax annualised earnings, MWC's interest in the partnership would command a market value of perhaps £65 million, i.e. less than one sixth the value at which it appears in these Accounts.

7. As a consequence of the accounting treatment for acquisitions and disposals, the book value of the intangible assets as a percentage of total assets is remarkably high and increasing as a result of the announced disposal programme. As at 31st March 1990, intangible assets (excluding those in the Macmillan/McGraw-Hill partnership) stood at £2.16 billion, representing more than 50% of gross assets and 215% of shareholders' equity at book value. If the intangible assets attributable to Macmillan/McGraw-Hill partnership are accounted for, intangible assets amount to £2.52 billion, representing 60% of gross assets and 250% of shareholders'

Maxwell Note – continued.

equity. In my opinion, it would be prudent for MWC to write down the intangible assets by amortizing goodwill. However, this would result in insufficent profit to pay a dividend - and the dividend is, of course, supporting the share price at its present level.

However, helpfully, the Annual Report and Accounts contains Canadian Shareholder Information which reconciles the financial statements to Canadian GAAP under which adjusted net earnings for the year ended 31st March 1990 are shown to be a loss of £97.9 million compared to a reported profit before extraordinary items of £126.8 million. Nearly all of the enormous difference may be explained by the Canadian GAAP principle of amortization of goodwill, resultant from acquisition,over ten years.

8. With adjustment of the non-recurring items and restating the financial statements to reflect a conservative acquisition accounting policy, MWC made a small loss compared with a reported profit of £101.1 million - see schedule of Maintainable Profits. If goodwill were amortized over ten years, the loss for the year ended 31st March 1990 would have been £207 million or 33 pence per share.

9. In its current financial situation, I consider MWC can no longer make large acquisitions and is now forced to dispose assets to repay debt. As a result, MWC's reported profits will fall dramatically and the company will not be able to maintain its dividend.

Maxwell Note – continued.

MAINTAINABLE PROFITS

£'s million

	Reported profit: Year ended 31st March 1990	Adjustments	Maintainable Profits (predicated)
Sales	1,242.1	-	1,242.1
Operating costs	(1,006.1)	(156.4)[a]	(1,162.5)
Other income	-	32.0[b]	32.0
Share of partnership/associates	25.2	-	25.2
	261.2		136.8
Exceptional item	19.2	(19.2)	-
Total operating profit	280.4		136.8
Net interest and investment income	(108.1)	(18.3)[c]	126.4
Profit before tax	172.3		10.4
Tax	(34.5)		(3.6)[d]
Profit after tax	137.8		6.8
Minority interests	(11.0)		(11.0)
Extraordinary items	(25.7)		-
Profit attributable to ordinary shareholders	101.1		(4.2)

Notes: a. Operating costs adjusted for provisions utilised of £83.4 million, property dealing profits of £41.0 million and transfers to other income of £32.0 million.

b. Transfer ot other income of items deducted from cost of sales, being publishing titles (£18.9 million), non-compete agreements(£6.2 million) and other income excluding property dealing profits of £6.9 million.

c. Reversal of net gains on sales of investments less provisions.

d. Tax is assumed to be at 35%.

Maxwell Note – continued.

MAX AA1548 Code MAX MAXAA1548

SEPON LIMITED

Shares 19,843,834

212 Sent / /
Replied 21/11/90

THE STOCK EXCHANGE
LONDON
EC2N 1HP

Reply Flag r

Update Flag

Print Flag P

Öááááááááááááá Beneficial Name ááááááááááááááááááááááááááááááááááá	Shares áááááá
GOLDMAN SACHS EQUITY SECURITIES (UK)	25,159,081
MCLEAN (R A) & CO LTD	2,408
AITKEN CAMPBELL & CO LTD	1,374

F4CMDHELP ESCEXIT F2SAVE Sh-F1TABLE F3VIEW F7DEL F8MODIFY F9QBE F10MULTI

Nominee
Sub Record 653 on Line 8 of 16

UBS PHILLIPS & DREW SECURITIES LTD	40,768
MORGAN STANLEY SECURITIES LTD	35,286
HOARE GOVETT SECURITIES LIMITED	32,448
NOMURA INTERNATIONAL LTD	21,682
SMITH NEW COURT SECURITIES PLC	195,304
S G WARBURG SECURITIES LTD	126,692
KLEINWORTH BENSON SECURITIES LTD	58,493
MAORGAN STANLEY SECURITIES LTD	8,303
DEWAAY SERVAIS & CIE S.C.S	3,000
LAWS & COMPANY LTD	12,500
DISCOUNT BANK & TRUST COMPANY	21,542
S.G. WARBURG & CO LTD	30,000
S.G. WARBURG SECURITIES (JAPAN) LTD	100,000

ááá

This print-out of the Sepon – registered holdings in Maxwell Communication Corporation shows the consequences of Goldman Sachs taking all the stock offered.

Stirring up Maxwell house

by MICHAEL WALTERS

WHAT are we to make of it? When the world looks grim and grey, and the boss advertises that he is ready to spend £45m to back his shares, is it a sign of strength? Or weakness?

It is a question which will have been troubling the dwindling band of shareholders in Robert Maxwell's Maxwell Communication Corporation.

It could be a big pay day for the panda-proportioned publisher on Friday. One of his companies is likely to have to pay over £45m to buy 30m shares in MCC at 152p each as a result of a put option he sold around the turn of the year.

Impressive stuff. Especially as the chaps who took the option (rumoured to be brokers Goldman Sachs) could have bought millions of MCC shares for between 135p and 145p. Unless they paid dearly for the option, selling them for 152p will yield a fat profit.

If the option is exercised, Maxwell will buy 4.6pc of MCC and take his family interest up to nearly 69pc. He did a similar deal which ran from August to November and gave him over 15m shares at 185p.

As a way of paying perhaps £5m or more over the odds, it looks a costly show of confidence. Why do it?

Clearly it helps support the MCC share price when Rupert Murdoch's troubles have raised doubts about heavily-borrowed publishing companies.

Will a similar new option be extended after Friday, covering the period around MCC's March 31 year-end? No one will say.

Room for manoeuvre may be limited. Much more family support might begin to jeopardise the company's place in the FTSE index of 100 top companies. Losing that would spark a round of selling from index funds. Without another option MCC shares could slide. Trading cannot be easy and profits for the six months to September raised a host of questions which will reappear with the full year's figures.

That £90m pre-tax half year profit was boosted by £45.7m of net exchange gains and included £15m from property development (against £32m previously).

It is not clear how long such profits can be sustained. A fall from £172m to £160m in annual profits might suggest underlying strength in difficult times. But perhaps not, given worries about the quality of the earnings.

At the half year borrowings were £1.9bn with talk of cutting debt by at least $750m (£375m) before the end of March. Asset sales have been sticky. In January the £60m sale of football stickers and album publisher Panini (announced in October) was called off.

Nothing much else has gone, though the Maxwell family is planning the Stock Exchange flotation of Mirror Group Newspapers in late spring/early summer. Unfortunately, the timing hardly suggests the family is dealing from strength.

The Gulf War has blown a hole in advertising revenue, already under pressure from the recession. Bankers Samuel Montagu reckon the float will not require a 1991 profit forecast, though they would expect some comfort over profits before going ahead.

THE company will take in the two Mirror newspapers, the Daily and Sunday Record in Scotland, plus the People — if that does not go to a management buy-out. It will also include the printing plants sold to the Mirror by MCC for £270m in June 1989.

The financial structure is unclear. The 1989 Mirror accounts show a £150m syndicated loan repayable by June 19, and since then, the group has spent £213m buying assorted assets (some at above market price) from MCC. That might suggest that the Mirror needs money, but Ian McIntosh at Montagu warns against paying much attention to the 1989 balance sheet. Much has changed since.

Mirror profits for 1990 might top £90m, and there are guesses that it could be valued at around £600m on flotation. If that includes the new money which is to be raised, it emphasises that floating the Mirror this summer is certainly selling low.

It is a sorry contrast for a company which paid high — an enviable 23 times earnings — when it bought the newspaper printing companies from MCC for £270m in June 1989.

Looking in the Mirror may not be so pretty, but MCC investors have done well by the £480m of assets they have sold to the Mirror since June 1989. And they may be pleased to see a little Mirror money flow into the private Maxwell coffers.

Who knows? The Maxwell Foundation, cosy behind the impenetrable company laws of Liechtenstein, may be looking strong, flush with cash.

But when MCC looks weak, and you are throwing option money around to buy the shares, every little helps.

***Daily Mail**, 12 February 1991.*

Globe-trotting Maxwell seeks a great escape

by MICHAEL WALTERS

ROBERT MAXWELL wanted me to leave. The two words were unmistakable, though not ones we would print in this newspaper. Nor ones that Maxwell would approve for the Daily Mirror.

That unexpected end to our last meeting raised questions about how he was coping with pressure. This is mounting day by day. It must be of great concern to investors in his two main quoted companies, Maxwell Communication Corporation and Mirror Group Newspapers.

He may emerge triumphant, master of a grand scheme to amaze us all. But it is becoming more difficult to imagine. The outlook for MCC, in particular, is growing steadily more uncertain.

So many Maxwell moves suggest he is weighed down with a heavy burden of debt, hampered by massive interest charges eating deep into operational profits. The Panorama programme on BBC TV on Monday touched many sensitive points, including the matter of the Goldman Sachs put options, originally raised here.

The Stock Exchange and the Department of Trade and Industry have been taking a long look at one of these. That ran from August last to November, and gave an unnamed party (assumed to have been American broker Goldman Sachs) the right to sell 15.65m MCC shares to Maxwell for 185p. That could have been hugely profitable, since Goldman could have bought MCC shares for as little as 140p and sold them to Maxwell for 185p.

This gave Goldman an incentive to buy MCC shares in eight weeks when Maxwell himself was not permitted to buy. Crucially, it helped stop MCC shares falling ever lower.

Dealers complained bitterly that they never knew what price, if any, Goldman had paid for the option. That obviously influenced what Goldman, which makes a market in MCC, could afford to pay for MCC shares and still make a profit.

The DTI will say nothing. Any criticism would be acutely embarrassing for Goldman and the Government. When scandal hit Salomon Brothers, Goldman stepped up to lead the US sale of the Government's next tranche of shares in British Telecom.

For Maxwell watchers, the possible significance of the Goldman option deal has moved more sharply into focus now.

Maxwell has pledged large numbers of shares in MCC and Mirror Group as security against loans. On some loans, extra security would be required if the value of the shares pledged fell below 145pc of the loan. So any fall in the MCC or Mirror Group shares might be important for Maxwell's private borrowings.

Last month, Goldman revealed it held nearly 5pc of MCC shares as security and almost 10pc of Mirror Group. And Robert Maxwell Holdings, a private Maxwell company, gave Midland Bank a legal charge over 13m Mirror Group shares on May 28, with another 27m pledged on July 26. The total debt in private Maxwell companies appears to be around £1bn.

THE public companies are also heavily in debt. MCC owes more than £1.3bn, and Mirror Group perhaps £160m. Maxwell told shareholders on September 11 that planned disposals would permit repayment of £450m of bank borrowings before March 31.

He also plans to split the North American business from the European companies, hoping that the two bits will somehow add up to three. Any split will not happen before February or March next year.

None of this helps confidence in a company which is under attack on other fronts. Panorama revisited arguments that the last reported MCC profits of £146m could be stripped back to £13m by knocking out exceptional and one-off items.

It also suggested intangible assets in the MCC balance sheet could be worth £1.5bn, not £2.1bn.

Maxwell is unimpressed by sceptics. But it is clear he bought companies galore when prices were high, and now must sell to cut debt when prices are depressed. A measure of his need can be gauged by the decision to float Mirror Group in May, when new issues were commanding a poor price and newspaper advertising revenues were depressed.

The float raised £200m for his private companies, yet within three months he had pledged 40m of the shares. He even sold his first love, the Pergamon scientific publishing business, to raise £440m for MCC.

At 167½p, MCC shares look highly vulnerable. It might not take much of a fall for them to lose their place in the FTSE 100 Share Index. Then the index-tracking investment funds would sell. That could trigger a sharper fall.

If there are still substantial private loans, secured against MCC shares, then a whole spiral of selling could start. Who knows where that would stop?

Daily Mail, 28 September 1991.

Why share dealings matter to Maxwell

by MICHAEL WALTERS

THERE is talk in the City about US broker Goldman Sachs' operations which appear to have helped sustain the share price of Maxwell Communication Corporation. Millions of shares have moved between Maxwell interests and Goldman, in one case without disclosure required by the Companies Act.

The Department of Trade and Industry has been studying a shareholder complaint about a £29m put option last year, one of two option deals giving Goldman the right to sell MCC shares to Maxwell interests.

It emerges that there was a third option deal, overlooked by the market, involving a Maxwell company buying a call option in 10m MCC shares. Directors may not buy options in shares of their companies. Surprisingly, the law allows purchases by companies controlled by such directors.

This 10m call option ran from March 30 to June 29 last year. Like the £29m put option on 15.65m shares, which lasted from August to November last year, each option helped support MCC's share price.

Some investors are upset that they did not appreciate the use of options in either deal. MCC simply said that Headington Investments, a Maxwell company, had acquired an interest. This was interpreted (wrongly) by many as indicating that the shares had already been bought.

In fact, MCC did send a second but little-noticed note to the Stock Exchange, indicating that the August-November deal involved a strike price of 185p, which suggested that one was an option deal.

Had investors better understood that Goldman had the right to sell MCC shares at 185p, they would have been reluctant to sell at 140p or less during October. One aggrieved investor threatens legal action against Goldman, whose part in the transaction was never publicly confirmed.

BBC's Panorama claimed that two Goldman accounts held substantial numbers of MCC shares on October 10. Goldman says they held much less than the 47m, or 7.3pc of MCC which Panorama suggests.

NORMALLY any holding over 3pc has to be published, but no stake was disclosed. Goldman would not have to announce holdings on the market-making book. The firm says it has revealed all that it was supposed to.

On November 30, the option was exercised, and a Maxwell company bought the 15.65m shares at 185p. How many shares did that leave in Goldman's hands?

Goldman soon had the chance of selling more to Maxwell interests. On January 7, 1991, Maxwell said he had sold another option allowing someone to sell 30m MCC shares to his interests at 152p on February 15. Again, Goldman appears to have been on the other end, and has not denied repeated claims that it was party to both put options. Maxwell's interests duly bought the 30m shares for £45m on February 15.

A study of market volume shows that in the six weeks when the option was known to be running, no-one could have bought more than 10.7m MCC shares through the market.

Did Goldman have the odd 30m in a back pocket? The option-terms would probably have covered the interest cost of holding the shares.

Whatever happened, that had the effect of stopping a potential sale to the market of 30m MCC shares.

By mid-February, Maxwell interests had plenty of cash to pay for 30m shares. As the option matured, Goldman bought 10pc of TF1, the largest TV channel in France from Pergamon Media Trust, part of Maxwell's private company empire. Goldman appears to have paid about £70m with a view to selling on.

Almost at once, Goldman and Maxwell interests were transacting business again, though no-one was to know until August 14.

Then a red-faced Goldman admitted that it was holding stakes worth £143m in MCC and Mirror Group Newspapers. Of that, £106m was held as security against loans to Maxwell interests. Nearly five months earlier, on March 27, Goldman had taken as collateral 4.79pc of MCC, worth over £60m.

Goldman had realised, very late, that 31.2m MCC shares should have been disclosed. It regretted a technical breach of the Companies Act.

In fact, the announcement indicated that Goldman also had other shares in MCC. It was interested in 7.5pc of MCC, or some 48.7m shares, valued in mid-August at £97m. Since then, the stake has been trimmed to 5.44pc.

All of this has to be seen against the role of Goldman day by day in MCC shares. Of the 11 market-makers in MCC, Goldman has frequently given the best prices in the largest amounts. That has supported the MCC price.

THIS is important to Maxwell. His private companies have borrowings of £1bn or so. Some are secured against MCC shares, and some require shares to the value of 145pc of the loan as security.

If the MCC price falls below a certain point, lenders might ask for their loans back, or require more shares as collateral.

In extreme cases, an MCC price fall could lead to lenders selling MCC shares. That could have a dramatic impact.

MCC shares are overshadowed by worries about heavy debt and the high proportion of profits from items other than normal trading. Confidence was not helped when chairman-elect Peter Walker declined to take up the post in July with the price around 190p.

Jean-Pierre Anselmini resigned unexpectedly as deputy chairman a week ago. Before he left, the shares were 186p. Now they are 159p.

Neither Mr Maxwell nor Goldman Sachs can be feeling comfortable.

Daily Mail, *11 October 1991.*

◆

CHAPTER FIVE

SHORT-SELLING (4)

◆

Investment analysis

This is not a book about investment analysis. But I think that it is important that one should hold accounts of targets and one should have a good idea of factors such as PE ratios for the target's sector and gearing that may prove acceptable (or not) to the market. Further, there are clear instances in the recent past when accounting practices offered the opportunity for a company to delude investors over many years. Certainly, "acquisition accounting" produced overstatement of profits for many companies until very recently (when a fresh, if different, set of absurdities has started to emerge). The previous chapter which covered Maxwell Communication Corporation, includes the note prepared in my office in respect of MCC. It shows that acquisition accounting obscured some important truths about MCC – although, and in fairness, the adjustments that could and should have been made by investors stared out of MCC's own accounts. For myself, I am not dogmatic about accounting standards. Even if they were to cost nothing to implement and audit, they are merely part of the language of business. And, since I would always argue that the purpose of language is to serve the user – even to the point where truth is purely a subsidiary or incidental objective, it follows (for me) that most time spent seeking perfection of accounting standards is time that is wasted. I would be impressed if the search for such perfection could be shown to reduce the incidence of fraud or encourage capital markets to operate more efficiently or cause business managers to apply funds to new projects on a more informed basis. But, since I see very little evidence (if any) of that, I would advocate saving the money spent on the search and subsequent changes, particularly as this money is currently levied in effect by a monopoly (because the companies that are audited cannot avoid audit and accounting standards).

You can skip this paragraph if you wish but, as a small digression, it seems to me that conflict is liberty. What this means is that by seeking to win an argument one prepares one's ground and thus reviews all one's strengths, weaknesses and opportunities. This process engenders liberty. Arguably, applying finer and finer standards in accounting constitutes the same beneficial process of achieving liberty. And politicians are duty-bound to arrange such a process for their people. It is just that the selection of the field of conflict can be to economic advantage. Accountancy products cannot be eaten and do not fall within this category.

The influence of the press and other commentators

Whether one is considering buying, buying to close, selling or short-selling, one has to be conscious of what the market is thinking (and then try to do the opposite or avoid following the crowd). As it happens I take all the UK quality press with the exception of the *Guardian.*

I was about to add that, whatever shortcomings may be identified in the *Guardian* for a short-seller, it is, of course, extraordinarily well written. But that would be to miss the point: which is that ever since the widely-reviled Rupert Murdoch decamped to Wapping, the quality UK press has improved beyond recognition with the possible exception of *The Times.* This improvement is also found in the financial pages. Inevitably, opinions there recorded affect share prices – particularly in active markets when punters are ready to follow the recommendations of newspapers.

I do not care to be dogmatic about the effect of other sources. For instance, when Cazenove decide on a view, they move the market through their trading. But they are not indiscreet. So they are not a source. Others are indiscreet when they should not be and so it has to be decided whether they are in breach of their obligations to their clients. If they are, one is legally as well as honour bound not to take advantage of their indiscretion. If they persist in being indiscreet, it makes you wonder whether they intend ultimately to deceive – a different proposition altogether!

I have taken tipsheets in my time. But the real advantage of a tipsheet is to draw the attention to an idea for further investigation or to enable one to go against the trend of the tipsheet so to close one's position. He who follows tipsheets to the letter will simply go bust or steadily waste his capital.

However, whether the information comes in written or oral form, it needs to be studied and weighed for quality and influence.

For instance, take a market report column in Spring 1995 which contained the advice that a certain firm of brokers considered that Tadpole Technology should be sold at 120p (the price was then 98p). The casual investor might remark that he should buy the stock on the grounds that it should not be sold until it is 120p. Of course, he might decide a moment later that his dealing expenses would be disproportionate to the limited upside he would here be considering. However, a reflective investor would surely decide that it is a rather odd firm of brokers that has clients holding the stock and yet which publicly limits their profits or recoveries. Accordingly, he will surely conclude that the brokers are probably really declaring that there is little upside and that the stock is quite possibly to be sold – particularly to those who are sufficiently ill-advised to buy (for whatever reason – one of which may be the suggestion that 120p is the selling point). I appreciate that all this may seem rather devious. But short-sellers who fail to engage in textual analysis will lose money.

Newspaper articles can be written in a perfectly responsible way. An example (I make no apology) is Michael Walters' article recommending Queen's Moat Houses (QMH), dated Monday, 22 May 1995. It was a perfectly fair and enthusiastic recommendation for what is in reality a very long-dated warrant at a seemingly low price. The article itself was part of a series that Michael has been writing for publication each Monday morning in the *Daily Mail.* Unsurprisingly, this series has built up a considerable following over the years. Equally unsurprisingly, private clients stormed for QMH ordinaries. By the end of that Monday they had more than doubled to 18.5p on volume of 37m – and it must be understood that they had been relisted the preceding Thursday at an opening price of 3p (to close at 6p) and had continued up another 3p on the Friday – volume was tens of millions on both days. I reflected upon the facts and read Tuesday's press which even suggested that some of the buying the previous day had been prompted by "corporate activity" (for which read takeover or long-term stakebuilding purposes).

All this seemed rather silly to me because any "corporate activity" deal could have taken place during the preceding three months – after all, QMH had been reconstructed over the preceding three years. It would be rather odd for the bidder to show his hand as soon as relisting had occurred. So that reason seemed to me to have caused misinformed buying on the Tuesday morning.

But I also judged that the public occasionally loves an investment name that has made it money in the past and/or where losses are to be recovered. QMH clearly fell within that category. So buyers were misjudging on that account.

Finally, Michael's article said BUY at 9p. It did not say BUY at 20p. And I am quite certain that Michael would never recommend buying a stock which had doubled on a Thursday, gone up by a further 50% on the Friday, and doubled yet again on the following Monday, if he were writing a column for publication on the following Tuesday. It was as clear an example of the crowd having gone mad as one could hope to identify in a typical year's trading. Further, there was a real bid by the market for stock. So, on behalf of myself and others, I short sold over 1m QMH at 19.5p and 20p. Within another fortnight, I had trousered over £50,000 profit. I swear to you that this was not difficult save in so far that there was an irritating delay through checking the conversion terms of part of the debt where, as it happens, I did not have a copy of the relisting documentation to hand.

Meeting dividend claims; some reflections upon Capital Gains Tax (CGT)

For many years, short-sellers could find a short-sold stock going ex-dividend prior to their closing. A debit would appear on one's statement months, perhaps many months, after one had bought to close (the happiest position arose – and still does – when the dividend was cancelled through a change of heart on the part of the company: closing bargains struck at the "ex-div" price stand and are not amended upwards). But the debit was only the net dividend. The national income figures were swollen to an extent by dividends that were never actually paid! Nowadays, although one is debited with not only the net dividend but, also, the related tax, the curious statistical effect remains. The tax just makes things a little more costly. Incidentally, it is interesting to note that the CGT legislation gives tax relief on the gross cost of dividends claimed – this gross cost is added on to the cost to close. There is no CGT indexation relief on the cost since the stock is not deemed to have been held for the minimum period required for indexation – this is despite the fact that inflation must work against the short-seller.

Stamp duty

In practice (but see Chapter Eight on Contracts for Differences), it is not possible for the private investor to avoid stamp duty on UK equities (excepting when they are purchased in ADR form) when buying to close. Given that stamp duty is a cost of acquisition, it is a little odd that one can be taxed on the purchase of something one never had and where a purchase is simply to close a short-sale.

I think the short answer is that stamp duty is not a tax on the fact of acquisition. It is in fact a tax on a document. That, as they say, is as may be. Government pronouncements have tantalised investors with the prospect of nil stamp duty. Indeed, such nirvana was promised if the LSE had been able to come up with an improved stock registration and bargain handling system. The project was known as Taurus. Its eventual abortion cost the market about £300m and stamp duty remains. I doubt if stamp duty will ever go. The Conservatives are the only party in the UK that has ever offered the hope of practical capitalism in action allied to lower taxation.

And they now seem to have given up on both those promises. Besides, the Government will need stamp duty to subsidise financially-failing regulatory bodies.

"Cashing and renewing": how it occurs and its converse, "renewing and cashing"; widening spreads on "renewing and cashing"

There was a time when stamp duty was refunded if a position was closed within the LSE account. That time was followed by the years 1986 to 1994 (in July 1994, account trading ceased) when stamp duty was not refunded on an account trade. However, under both regimes, buyers faced the requirement to settle on the settlement day for that particular account. Since that entailed putting up cash, some investors simultaneously sold in the current account and bought back their position for the new account and, because the bargains were matched, the market-maker's turn, although most certainly there, was less than the "touch". There was also an imputed charge for the market-maker to finance the position.

The effective rate of interest was outrageous and that was true whether the stamp duty was refunded or not. I have some small sympathy with the market-makers – after all, they are entitled to categorise an investor's buy order as speculative and inadequately financed. They are entitled to sell stock in the market generally in the belief that he who has bought speculatively will dump the stock fairly shortly afterwards. If, then, this stock is denied to the market through its being carried over to a later account, the market-maker will find himself short of stock. That said, he doesn't half know that there is a compulsory seller out there.

This process was known as "cashing and newing". The "newing" bit is now redundant because the "new" of "newing" referred to the new account.

And there is no more account trading. That said, investors can buy on deferred terms and they may wish to renew their positions. So I suppose that "cashing and newing" will persist. Without wishing to bore everybody, I suppose it could be called "cashing and renewing".

Of course, its converse, only encountered by the short-seller, must be known as "renewing and cashing". Given that the market is not financing the stock, the market-maker's dealing turn should be approaching non-existent. It often is not.

Again, there is a curious feature which arises with the approaching suspension of a quotation. If this is seen as likely, the market-makers appreciate that those seeking to "renew and cash" stand to make a lot of money. Therefore, the market-makers tend to widen their dealing turn on the renewal. One would have thought that competition would inhibit this process. But it does not. In their defence, once suspension has occurred, your broker becomes their counterparty and thus, under the minimum capital requirements with which all professionals in the market must cope, capital is absorbed – the widening of spreads is the only way to cope with this problem in advance. The trouble is the extra thus charged is grotesquely excessive when compared with any conceivable discounted cost of risk.

Adjustment of requirements to close in the event of intervening scrip or rights issues

These adjustments are simply a matter of equitable sense. In the event of a scrip issue, when (say) a further share is issued for each one held, you simply need to deliver two shares for each one sold.

Rights issues are a little more complicated. Here, you must buy nil paid rights to cover your sale contract. After all, the buyer of the cum rights stock that you sold has rights. And nobody bar you is going to ensure them.

You buy them and deliver them to the market. But, if you do not, you will eventually be debited with the cost of fully paid new shares less the amount payable on subscription. Put another way, you will be "bought-in".

Other things being equal, the ex-rights price will be at a discount roughly equal to the rights value. And, while the cash profit available through buying to close the original sale is to hand on a T + 5 basis, the requirement for cash when buying nil paid rights is on a cash settlement basis. This means that you may be required to put up cash for which you had not otherwise budgeted.

Further, it is generally best to leave the purchase of nil paid rights as late as possible. This is because there are always some investors who hold rights yet foolishly hope that some windfall will provide the cash to allow the new shares to be taken up. They tend to sell late. Another consideration is that the issuers of these new shares tend artificially to manipulate upwards the ex-rights price for as long as possible to encourage as many takers as possible and, no doubt, to reassure those who have underwritten the issue. However, this process comes to an end as the issue closes. It is at that moment that the most favourable buying opportunity may be expected to arise. I need hardly add that, sometimes, those who handle such an issue regard it as attractive and artificially manipulate the price down so that they can pick up shares cheaply at the end of the rights quotation period or through stock put on them as a result of the underwriting.

On balance, I favour buying nil paid rights in order to control the price paid. I dislike leaving a position open such that I am bought-in unless I am tolerably sure that there is a further fall to come – "renewing and cashing" would then apply. But you should not leave buying nil paid rights so late that the renounceable letter of allotment that you have bought cannot get through your broker's office to the market which originally bought your sale cum rights. You should discuss that with your broker.

There is a variation where new shares are issued in terms of an open offer and clawback. Here there is no trading of nil paid stock. The value of the right of a subscriber to the new stock is not transferable. However, if you have short-sold stock which is cum the right to participate in the open offer (the "ex-offer" quotation normally follows within twenty–four hours of the offer being announced), the buyer has a claim in the normal manner. Therefore he can insist that you deliver stock. He in turn must pay you what he would have paid by way of subscription. This is done through the market. There is a chance that he will not bother since the value achieved may be too small or potentially non-existent. It is entirely at his option.

Price stabilisation: what it means for short-sellers

Unless you work in the market, are a fund manager or on the board of a substantial quoted company, you are probably unaware of how share prices are manipulated over long periods at the bidding of the boards of main shareholders in quoted companies. For instance, a major new issue will usually be handled by a City stockbroker who will undertake that, within reason, the share price of the issue will not substantially underperform relative to the market or the client's sector for as much as two years after the issue. The expenses of this operation (brokers do not do it just for commission/lunch money – they feel a need for a luxurious dinner coming on) are borne by the client company. This enables larger shareholders to be accommodated should they seek an exit and it also makes it much harder for professional advisers to face proceedings for incompetence or negligence or worse on the run up to the issue. Why this expense should be borne by, in effect, all shareholders, many of whom are blissfully unaware of its existence, I have not the faintest idea. After all, it is an expense that does not assist the trade/profits of the company. It is an expense to keep the big cheeses even bigger.

The consequence of this is that it is very hard to expect a price to break down soon after a flotation. That said, I would not say that such a break down cannot happen. In fact, there were a number of break downs in prices of new issues in 1994. If I had to guess why, the new issue market of 1994 was so frothy that director shareholders were frequently able to sell substantial parts of their holdings at the time of the flotation. Besides, price stabilisation has to face reality. It cannot suppress wholesale unpalatable truth. And there were a fair number of unpalatable truths in the 1994 new issue after market.

Time/risk exposure

The longer that you stay short, the greater your risk of a major loss. This will sound a strange caveat in the light of my urging you to buy as much time as possible to stay short.

Information comes from all angles

As in life in general, one must always keep an open mind for fresh information. Information on the long-term long tack arrives and should be acted upon without delay. But should you judge that it is sound, you can sit back. You may even go on holiday. However, information on the short-tack can vitally impact with very little notice. It might be on the television news at 10.00 p.m. – too late for newspaper City desks to air the matter properly in the following day's papers. Thus a classic arbitrage of ignorance arises. This arbitrage is immediate.

Information might come from a court case moving unexpectedly against your target. Most people are amazingly slow to evaluate the consequences of judicial decisions. And, once they get round to them, they overreact. It is a tremendous opportunity for the trader.

Sadly, some information received from respectable news services is not merely late, it is wrong either in fact or in tone. Although it seems to come with the stamp of authority, it is actually misleading. To react quickly to that is vital. For instance, in late 1993, Automated Security Holdings announced inter alia that it had suffered a £32m exceptional loss. An hour or so later, during which period directors were free to deal and, indeed, bought, the loss was corrected down to £2m. I wish I were in a position to be so casual with a typewriter.

Arbitraging different classes of capital

The opportunity to arbitrage as between different classes of capital rarely arises. Although LSE market-makers are quite extraordinarily overpaid, they rarely let an opportunity slip. So it is difficult for someone who is not a market-maker to benefit – additionally, it will be borne in mind that someone who is not a market-maker faces substantial expenses not faced by the market-maker. But the opportunities do arise and it is both satisfying and worthwhile to spot the moment.

For instance, in November 1993, a small company, NMC had warrants which fell to be converted for the last time by paying a further 16p per share to derive an ordinary then around £1.10. As it happens, I was bullish towards NMC so I bought about 100,000 warrants at around 90p onwards.

Warrants tend to become available just before the final conversion date because warrant holders do not have the money to effect the conversion or, if they do, they do not really want to stay on with the fully paid ordinary shares. They regard the approach of the final conversion date as a moment to leave the party. That is how I was supplied. It is also the case that many investors usually regard any proceeds from sales of warrants as pure profit because the warrants that they hold were issued for free earlier in the company's life. It all depends on what you define as free.

Since I was already over invested in NMC – I had 97,500 warrants before this arbitraging started – I tended to keep short-selling NMC ordinary shares to cover the additional warrants that I had purchased.

One effect of the warrant purchases was to try and persuade the market that there might be a sustained demand for the ordinary shares. This tended to push up the price of the ordinary shares – which made for a higher price at which I could short-sell the ordinaries. So, not surprisingly, that was the order in which I executed the trades.

In the absence of an imminent conversion date it is generally unwise to try this arbitrage/short-sell strategy. This is because the theoretical tradeable gap does not necessarily close – indeed it is nearly always certain that the time value in the warrant price will not merely inhibit a trade, it will prohibit it. Of course, the bulk of the NMC warrants could not have been delivered by the market in time for me to meet the deadline for conversion (at which point the warrants would have been worthless). So, where I did not hold a certificate, I asked my broker to ask the market to convert the warrants to ordinary shares and to debit me with the subscription of 16p per share. I then completed delivery to cover my short-sold position. It was worth an average 5p per share profit clear of expenses and risk-free. In short, £5,000 for no work at all.

A wholly unexpected bonus arose because as I never took delivery of the bulk of these warrants from the market, I was refunded the stamp duty on their acquisition, about £500. I call that breakfast, lunch and dinner money.

CASE STUDY:
Tiphook

My first short-sale of Tiphook (in late 1991) was at 8p below its all-time high of £5.80. I would like to be able to claim that that this was through some outstandingly shrewd judgement on my part. But it was not. It was simply a friend of mine being friendly one morning when he had nothing better to do. Of course, I should really only have gone along with the trade after having done my own homework. I suppose I was just being idle.

But I immediately got hold of a set of accounts and a tell-tale point stared out: the company had declared that there was no chance of obsolescence in its container fleet. Well, maybe. And I suppose that such is a handy claim if one is seeking to justify depreciation rates of the order of 5% or, even 4% p.a. But, surely, the history of the twentieth century is one of massive technological change. I suppose Tiphook's (then) confidence was the sort displayed by owners of ocean-going cargo vessels in the late 1940s – who, no doubt, opined that their trade would be immune from change – only to see it transformed a few years later by, of course, containers. So I questioned the depreciation charge because the company's conduct struck me as foolish.

I was also aware that the chief executive of Tiphook, in high public profile, was associated with the Conservative Party and, also, the Royal Family (through the Prince's Trust). Now, I am not knocking either of those institutions. They are doing it famously well for themselves in any event. But companies are in business to make money. They are not in business to provide cash for lavish headquarters and associations. Still less are they served by executive jets. Tiphook had all of these. Further, at the time of my sale, Tiphook had just completed its listing arrangements in New York. As some cynics will confirm, this process is invariably preceded by a "road show" to see the stock well held in ADR form. It is inevitably followed by a period of consolidation.

Curiously, and by one of those happy coincidences in life, Tiphook's management, rather than deal directly with points put by analysts, appointed a public relations officer, called Sue E.Ville (no relation of Cruella de Ville). It was both a warning and a laugh. Incidentally, some months later, I telephoned and asked Ms Ville for copies of the accounts of two American competitors of Tiphook, namely Excel Corp and Gat-X. My purpose was to consider their ratings and that accorded to Tiphook. She advised that Tiphook "does not talk to people like you". Well, it has now!

At the time of writing, the company has changed its name to Central Trailer Rental, Mr Montague has gone bankrupt and the shares are comfortably under 50p. The jury is still out.

CASE STUDY:
Amber Day

I was first warned about Amber Day in mid-1991. The caller did not specify what was wrong. He merely said that there were rumours. If one were to trade on all such "tips" one would rapidly go bust. But, since the caller was and is well-informed and not given to malice, I naturally put Amber Day on the short-sell list. It was not until Christmas 1991 that I was again pressed to trade. By then, the stock had hit an all-time peak of 130p (capitalising the company at around £150m) and had slipped back to about 110p. But a conversation with a journalist revealed that it was seriously claimed by Amber Day itself that a fair rating would be 300p – at a time when the disclosed net tangible assets per share were of the order of 20p. Even if the figure of 300p was merely a target it was completely unrealistic. And any management that is unrealistic should be sold immediately. So I did.

I understand that the then management of Amber Day came to blame me for the decline in the price of Amber Day. But the truth behind the decline is more prosaic. Quite simply, the maintainable profits to be expected from the company were not there so even the foothills of 300p could not be contemplated. This was so because the accounts spoke for themselves. Further, the company's principal business, What Everyone Wants (now Amber Day's name), was and remains discount retailing. Now, I am all for discount retailing since it cuts out the flim-flam men who put a business's overheads up to no purpose. But the business itself has a limited appeal and has no monopoly quality like (say) a wonder drug or a cobalt mine. So 300p was never on the cards.

As it happens, WEW has fallen on hard times. It has yet to recover. Arguably, if you adjust for cash raised since 1992 in the form of rights issues, WEW has been to a nil valuation since I started my bear-raid.

Bear raiders drive equities down

THE MARKET

By Paul Murphy

IF THE pessimists wanted any further excuse to mark prices lower, they might turn to the latest Minet Consultancy confidence index—a toe-dip of institutional sensitivities undertaken quarterly by the big Minet fund management group.

It shows, perhaps alarmingly, that fund managers have a new overlord: the actuary.

It seems that "with-profits" insurance policy funds have been asked by their in-house number-crunchers to avoid speculative shares and switch instead to the copper-bottomed yields offered by gilts—a trend which equity and fixed interest salesmen have suspected for weeks.

On top of this comes the worries over Lloyd's members.

Ask a salesman about the market's prospects during the remainder of the year and he or she will point to the Wellcome Trust offer of about £3 billion in Wellcome stock. If the offer goes well, there will be £3 billion to re-invest, which should naturally push top stocks sharply higher.

But Lloyd's members have to stump up £2 billion in two payments—one at the end of July, the other in September. No one knows what portion of these funds are in shares, but informal guesses say "quite a lot". In short, even the best lateral thinking bull marketeers can quickly find themselves matched by the bears. The Wellcome fund injection could turn out to be a rather short-lived high.

On the subject of bears, one raider was on the phone yesterday morning selling Spring Ram hard. The line was that Spring Ram (whose market capitalisation has risen from £11m to over £500m in nine years) has now gone "ex-growth". He picked his time. Chairman Bill Rooney is holiday, while the rest of the board were in meetings yesterday which were said to be continuing this morning. But Stuart Greenwood, finance director, explained that, while the company no longer believes it can "'walk on water" (it achieved rates of 50pc annual compound growth in the 1980s), the market consensus still says it will turn in a 20pc rise this year, despite the recession. "The only thing to do with these so-called bear-raiders is to catch them and give them a quick kick in the knee," Mr Greenwood suggests. The stock fell 7 to 133p on a "better cut than get caught" basis.

Wellcome, meanwhile, looked positively sick. Initially, this was put down to a statement on Glaxo's anti-Aids research (a theoretical potion called 3TC) delivered at the big Aids conference in Amsterdam. Later, dealers began to talk of the re-emergence of a couple of big short sellers in the market, heartened by news that the offer seems to be going relatively well. If the sellers are sure the offer is not going to grind to a halt, they can be relatively sure they will be able to buy back stock cheaper in the not-too-distant future. Slumping to a new low for the year of 839p, **Wellcome** eventually closed 25 adrift at 845p.

The market as whole remained nervous throughout the day. Large Friday falls in New York and Tokyo convinced dealers in London that they had best ward off any possible wave of sellers here by marking prices sharply lower first thing.

With the FT-SE 100 off almost 30 points at the outset, the sellers subsequently failed to materialise and somthing of a rally was attempted mid-morning.

Then the boys in the futures pits took hold. Frenetic activity was reported over lunch-time as dealers debated the future of sterling and took bets on the chances of a half-point rise in interest rates and/or the so-called "double-dip" recession. Punters were even said to be digging out their charts of the 1929 crash and its five-year aftermath. That, too, was a big boom followed by a big slump and share prices fell further and quicker during the early 1930s than in the immediate aftermath of the crash.

Without any new news to drive it, the market plummeted, and the main Footsie cash index stood almost 65 points down at one stage at 2367·1. Later, dealers decided price-cutting had been overdone and the braver equity strategists started to talk of the historically low ratio between equities and gilts—simply suggesting that the market had been oversold.

The odd appearance of a bargain hunter with cash in his hand coincided with the heavy round of central bank intervention against the German mark. Such a combination soon had the index on the mend. The 2400 level was eventually established as something of a support level and the Footsie's final reading came in at 2403·7, down 28·2.

Those stocks which found themselves under pressure on Friday (dollar-earners, together with the consumer and building sectors) were again under the cosh. **Tomkins** lost a further 15 to 441p, **Siebe** shed 11 to 662p, **Whitbread "A"** fell 13 to 399p and **Body Shop** moved from 300p to 291p. **Amber Day** ended at is year's low, down 2 at 35p while **Alexon**, another fashion house, fell 5 to 197p.

Tarmac (down 5½ at 73½p) and Pilkington (steady at 99p) both saw heavy volumes. Punters were quick to note that the market has lost more than 12pc since May when several of the big acquisitive conglomerates suggested the prices of target companies were much too high. Both have been widely tipped as potential takeover stocks.

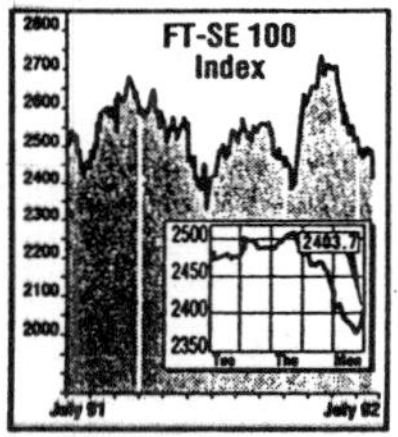

MAIN PRICE CHANGES

Rises: 69 **Falls:** 862 **Unchanged:** 743

RISES		
Lasmo	131	+6
Mirror Group	58½	+5½
Transfer Tech	405	+10
FALLS		
Barclays	305	−10
British Aerospace	215	−27
Cadbury	475	−14
Cardiff Property	80	−23
Davies & Newman	24	−12
General Accident	387	−17
Kingfisher	437	−11
Northern Foods	584	−19
P & O	362	−12
Proteus	337	−41
Wellcome	845	−18

The Daily Telegraph, *21 July 1992. Evil Knievil at work on Spring Ram.*

CASE STUDY:
Spring Ram

The Ram of Spring Ram is derived from Mr **R**ooney **A**nd Mr **M**urray, the company's founders; and short-selling Spring Ram was colossal fun. One reason was that the maximum practical position to take was about 100,000 shares – the market would not happily deal at the touch in more and I was easily sufficiently solvent to cope with any vicissitudes that might arise on an exposure of the order of £125,000.

Unlike many other shorting operations, this started not so much from any particular words or use of words in the accounts although there were a number of most interesting points therein. It started with the sheer silliness of the December 1991 accounts which was full of drawings of chaps sprinting off in running races. Well, I might have accepted this general sprinting off for excellence had the business been the manufacture/distribution of running shoes or of cream to prevent athlete's foot. But Spring Ram's business was builders' merchants' and DIY supplies. And, even though it is a sound policy for a company to use the glossiness of its accounts as an aid to sales – customers frequently warm to a supplier's claim to professionalism by reacting favourably to its accounts – there is a limit. Spring Ram's accounts were staggeringly and exaggeratedly glossy. To me, the presentation of the accounts looked to be trying to hide an altogether different state of affairs.

Further, a friend in the bathroom equipment business advised me that Spring Ram was slow to pay its bills. This should not happen in the case of a company that has tens of millions of pounds in cash in its balance sheet. Another friend, in the interior decoration business, advised me that he had always thought Spring Ram's margins wholly incredible since they were maintained and improved during the stiffest recession for some years. Accordingly, I reckoned that Spring Ram was a natural short-sell candidate.

I did not catch the top (it is always hard to catch either a top or a bottom), which was £1.81, achieved in May 1992. But my first sale was of 50,000 shares at £1.38 on 20 July 1992. Paul Murphy, who wrote the market report for the *Daily Telegraph*, even reported that I, in concert with others, had picked my selling moment because Mr Rooney had gone on holiday (see page 107). After all, given that Sir Winston Churchill opined that he could not think of a better time to kick a man than when he is down (this was in response to the plea that it would be the worst time) it follows that it is good practice to mount a bear-raid when there is no supremo around to give the best story in the company's support.

Actually, I did not get Rooney to take the mickey out of me (well, what else would you expect from a Rooney set upon restoring his name?). Instead, the *Daily Telegraph* market report was advised by the finance director, one Stuart Greenwood, that "the only thing to do with these so-called bear-raiders is to catch them and give them a quick kick in the knee". I put this down to a Yorkshireman's sense of repartee. So I sold another 75,000 shares – this time at £1.31. I put it about that I had purchased some knee-cap covers and a supply of Corton Charlemagne in case I were to find myself hospitalised. Somehow, Paul got this story as well.

I have elsewhere in this book considered how brokers support the share prices of their corporate clients. The economics justify their doing so. But this tendency causes even quite sensible stockbrokers to persist too long in support. And I must judge that this was the case over Spring Ram. A Mr Pat O'Reilly of stockbrokers, Panmure Gordon, was then (and, as far as I am aware, remains) a well-regarded judge of market affairs. But, for whatever reason, he declined publicly to admit the possibility that Spring Ram was doing less well than it was claiming. He said to the *Yorkshire Evening Post:* "It's a seller's market at the moment. Spring Ram has been so successful in recent years that it has a number of rivals that would like to see it struggle. It's very easy for people to say that the company is struggling just because it isn't doing as well this year as in previous years. In fact, it is doing extremely well considering the economic climate."

The *Yorkshire Post* wrote: "One rogue dealer was reported to have wiped £30m off a Bradford firm's (i.e. Spring Ram's) value and made a packet". I take this reference to be to myself because of the newspaper's reference to "his having collected hundreds of thousands of pounds....P&O, Ratners and Brent Walker" – and that, however incorrect a description of what I had actually done, was derived from a *Sunday Times* article of eighteen months earlier – and that article was based on me. To me, it seems a lurid use of "rogue". Surely, the better word is "effective".

But the more interesting aspect of the article is the tenor of Mr O'Reilly's remarks. One needs to be fairly careful before accepting points reported in this manner – although, in my experience, reporters are usually meticulous when reporting sources verbatim. First, although it was indeed a "seller's market", it was not that much of a seller's market – sentiment was beginning to turn to the bull tack. And a broker of Mr O'Reilly's experience knew or ought to have known that that was the case. So his opening remarks did not feel entirely right to me. There seemed to be a hidden agenda. Secondly, it is extraordinarily stupid to mislead the market on the bear tack because (i) it is a criminal act to do so – see the section on FSA 1986 S47 and (ii) there is little likelihood of profit – certainly by relation to that from perfectly readily identified over-promoted stocks elsewhere in the market. So, Mr O'Reilly's remarks that the rumours surrounding Spring Ram could be attributed to jealous rivals did not seem sound. Jealous rivals might have spread them. But the rumours originated elsewhere. I discounted Mr O'Reilly.

But I had bought to close at £1.24 on 23 July 1992 and, in a sense, was indifferent to the move back up as Panmure Gordon's clients purchased. So, on 27 July 1992, I sold 50,000 shares at £1.28. I do not want to bore readers with a blow by blow account. So I have shown separately my dealings in Spring Ram for the whole of 1992 on page 112. Readers will see that, although there was a useful profit the dealing expenses were phenomenal.

Although this schedule of dealings suggests a general decline in the share price of Spring Ram, the truth is that it oscillated quite considerably. After my purchase at £1.22 on 3 September, the price recovered to about £1.35 or more. However, in early November, Spring Ram finally announced the first of a series of warnings. This was referred to on 18 November by Paul Murphy in the *Daily Telegraph:* "With an excruciating pun at the ready ('the silence of the Rams'), the bear-raiders are back stalking Spring Ram. They gave the stock a good spanking in late July, boldly suggesting the home improvement firm had gone ex-growth and talking darkly of accounting irregularities. Sources at Spring Ram rubbished such talk at the time only to come clean earlier this month when the company launched a bid for Stag Furniture. Although the shares have lost more than 30% since the truth about problems at Spring's Balterley Bathrooms subsidiary emerged, the raiders reckon the management are getting off too lightly. Even loyal supporters of Spring Ram concede that some form of independent check on the accounts would help clear the air. The bears say that they are stunned at the board's indifference to the falling share price and are selling short in the belief that some parties in the possession of accurate inside information are already off-loading stock." Said it all, really.

Today, Spring Ram, despite the market in general having risen some 20% since the events here described, stands below 40p and Mr Rooney and Mr Murray have left the company. The fact is that, when a company is shown to be less than its claims, its share price performance is not merely as leaden as its contemporaries, it is usually much worse. Trouble is rarely cleaned up overnight.

BOUGHT				SOLD			
Date	Quantity 000's	Price p.	Consideration £	Date	Quantity 000's	Price p.	Consideration £
20/7	50	133	66,500	20/7	50	138	69,000
23/7	75	124	93,000	23/7	75	131	98,250
				27/7	50	128	64,000
				31/7	50	118	59,000
				3/8	25	117	29,250
4/8	50	110	55,000				
				5/8	50	111	55,500
7/8	50	105	52,500				
10/8	25	108	27,000				
				12/8	50	120	60,000
3/9	100	122	122,000				
6/11	20	115	23.000	6/11	20	122	24,400
6/11	30	120	36,000	6/11	30	123	36,900
				9/11	30	117	35,100
				13/11	30	115	34,500
18/11	30	108	32,400				
18/11	30	106	31,800				
				2/12	50	100	50,000
3/12	50	93½	46,750				
	510		585,950		510		615,900
Brokerage on average 0.25%			1,465	Brokerage on average 0.25%			1,540
Stamp duty to close 0.5%			2,930				
PROFIT FOR 1992			**£27,095**				
			£617,440				£617,440

Spring Ram: Evil Knievil's dealings, 1992.

CHAPTER SIX

TRADITIONAL & TRADED OPTIONS

Definitions, calls and puts*

> * For a complete introduction to this subject, readers are advised to study *Traded Options – A Private Investor's Guide* by Peter Temple, sponsored by the London International Financial Futures and Option Exchange (LIFFE) and ProShare Limited: see Appendix Two for full details.

There are two sorts of option to buy (call) or sell (put) an equity. One is the traditional three-month option which is purchased from or sold to an option dealer. These have been available since before the Napoleonic wars. The other sort is a traded option, quoted by market-makers for standardised striking prices and delivery dates. Whereas the latter is a visible market, the former is very far from that.

A means of selling stock is to write a traditional call option or sell a traded call option. There are two problems for the private investor. Forgetting the requirements for collateral, selling a traded call option means selling a heavily researched stock and, as a general rule, I dismiss that in terms of the section on short-selling leaders. To write a traditional option, you need to find somebody to buy one. That is rather like selling tickets to Glyndebourne outside Wembley: you might succeed in achieving one sale but it is nearly certain that, after standing around for a couple of hours, your time might be judged better expended elsewhere!

That said, it happens. As a general rule the option dealers (there are currently only two in London – this means grossly inadequate competition) take all the business that is worth having. Even so, every now and then, they let some spill over. It is worth being ready.

As noted above, the drawback about traditional options is that there is no proper or visible market in them. So, for nearly all short-sale targets, the only approach is to short-sell them in the normal manner. For that is the only way to get a keen price in your stock.

Giving for the put and taking for the call, the "push me, pull you" – an alternative to short-selling

Generally speaking, conventional traditional and, sometimes, traded put options are too expensive. There is too little competititon in the provision of traditional options and, thus, the charge for the "time value" is disproportionate. But one has to recognise that a conventional short-sale will be bought-in by the LSE central clearing house within three to, possibly, seven weeks of the sale. A way to lengthen this period is to purchase a put option from an option dealer (as noted above, there are currently only two in

London) but request that he simultaneously buys a call option from you. Of course, this will be for a consideration which is a little less than that which you paid for the put and there is the unhappy difficulty that it is hard to fine-check the option dealer's assertion that the strike price at which, in effect, you are selling is actually the touch – it will be recalled that on the down tack it is very much in an option dealer's interest to reduce the strike price.

Nor is that all: should you choose to exercise your put option to sell to enable you to buy before the twelve week traditional option period expires, you remain open on the call that you have granted. It is possible to persuade the option dealer to void his call option at the same time that you exercise your put. But option dealers are not paid to be kind to you and one should not bank on sympathetic treatment. Brokerage is payable in respect of both aspects (ie. the put and call considerations) of the "push me, pull you" and negotiation may bring the rates down. Many firms of brokers will not contemplate such transactions because they cannot control or understand them.

The really important point to recognise is that adopting a "push me, pull you" exposes you to quite as much risk as a conventional short-sale. Further it may well cost more. The principal advantage is that a greater period is assured before you are circumscribed by a buying-in notice.

CASE STUDY:
Using A Traded Option To Short-Sell

As considered elsewhere in this book, it is unusual to find a glaring short-sell candidate in a FT-SE 100 constituent because it is bound to be closely researched and thus not likely to give a trading opportunity. Further, although Jim Slater has remarked that elephants do not gallop, I think he would also agree that they hardly ever dive off a cliff. But, from time to time, it is correct to attack a FT-SE constituent and traded options are attractive because dealing costs can be enormously reduced by selecting a date some nine months ahead and selling the call option. For the purpose of this illustration, I have assumed a FT-SE constituent, Bourbon PLC (which like elephants, forgets nothing but, unlike elephants, learns nothing – in short, its star is declining).

Current (Day one, Month one) price of Bourbon PLC is 800p. The quotation in Bourbon 750p calls for option settlement nine months into the future is 100p to 105p – here taken as 102.5p. Note that there is 50p of intrinsic value and 52.5p of time value. Space restriction does not permit the calculation for fair value having regard to volatility, interest rates, likely dividend levels and ex-dividend dates. You have decided to short-sell 100 contracts of (or 100,000 shares in) Bourbon PLC month 9 800p calls. You will receive a contract note as follows:

CLEANANDS ANONEST, Lunnun Wall St., EC2
(LIFFE CLEARING MEMBER FIRM OF STOCK AND SHARE BROKERS)

Sold by order of A.N. Opportunist:

100 Month 9 Bourbon PLC 800p calls @ 100p Proceeds: £100,000.00

Less:	Liffe Clearing charge @ £2.50 per contract	£250
	Brokerage/commission as agreed	£200
	Net proceeds	£99,550

It is important to note that, since you have no intention of owning Bourbon PLC shares, you cannot bank this money – even though it will be held by the broker earning interest for you. You will be required to put up collateral (cash or gilts) of the order of 30% of the outstanding position. That is a small matter of 30% of 100,000 times 800p or £240,000. Not everybody keeps this sort of money in cash or near cash.

A month or two later, and after you have entertained a coterie of journalists at The Connaught, you are not surprised by a shock horror story to the effect that Bourbon PLC is encountering trading uncertainties. The result is that the ordinary price declines to 750p. You decide to close your position. You will receive a contract note as follows:

CLEANANDS ANONEST, Lunnun Wall St., EC2
(LIFFE CLEARING MEMBER FIRM OF STOCK AND SHARE BROKERS)

Bought by order of A.N. Opportunist

100 Month 9 Bourbon PLC 800p calls @ 60p	£60,000
Add: Brokerage/commission as agreed	£200
	£60,200
Profit on transaction	£30,350

This is not a book on traded options. However, whether writing calls or puts, one should bear in mind that the holder of a call option can call the stock for delivery at any time (although he is unlikely to do so given the fact that he would have to pay 800p earlier than he need do) while the holder of a put can put stock on the writer because the holder has judged that the stock has bottomed and that he can profitably buy to close.

* * *

◆

CHAPTER SEVEN
TRADING IN FUTURES

◆

FT-SE 100

As noted elsewhere, it is far too expensive for a holder of equities to sell all of them on the argument that the market is about to decline 10% – and then top up with a few short sales for good measure. He would very probably be wrong about the extent of the fall by the time he has to buy them back. And, even if he were not, his dealing costs would be prodigious.

The only effective manner of trading on the view that the market is about to decline generally is to buy put options on the FT-SE 100 index or, better, write call options. It is better because the market usually pays more to the writer rather than the purchaser of an option. The transaction costs are low in relation to the exposure sought. For instance, one might purchase an option to sell the FT-SE at 3,000 points four weeks hence for 50 points. Brokerage varies. But you can expect to negotiate a brokerage of 1% or (as in this instance) 0.5 points (there is no stamp duty) – this is one six thousandth of the underlying "stock".

The market-maker's turn might be (only he knows) a further 2 points and brokerage to close (if a closing bargain is struck) is another 0.5 points. All told, 3 points on 3,000 or one thousandth of the underlying "stock" is a tiny fraction of the costs to sell and repurchase a typical FT-SE 100 constituent – those might total between 2% to 3%. Further, where the futures contract is allowed to run to expiry (but see below) there is no brokerage on the closing bargain – this makes a FT-SE 100 trade even cheaper.

The trouble is that it is extremely hard to know which way the FT-SE 100 is going. We have all read how Bernard Baruch called the 1929 collapse almost to a day. We all know that Sir James Goldsmith went 100% liquid just before October 1987. But, for most mortals, such insight is not available. The truth is that the futures market is only traded by well-informed individuals. Thus, it is not possible for the ordinary investor seriously to contemplate anything other than an insurance transaction – whereas, of course, the short-seller short-term trader must take more out of the market than he puts in taking one year with another. That is hard.

Indeed, the future often seems to have a life of its own. There are standard adjustments for the future contract's run to expiry in respect of interest foregone (through being in the FT-SE 100 rather than cash) and ex-dividend dates. But the price actually quoted frequently differs by up to 25 points or more from the expected or theoretical futures price. When this happens, one can forecast with some confidence that the cash or underlying stockmarket is about to catch up in whatever direction is prognosticated. For, nowadays, the cash market is wagged by the future – after all, it is so much cheaper to deal in the future. However, one should be cautious of confident FT-SE 100 forecasts. They are so often wrong. One should beware of him who remarks "I have seen the future and it works".

An interesting feature of FT-SE 100 trading is that it is settled by reference to a make-up figure which is determined by noting the best bid and the best offer in each FT-SE 100 constituent at the end of each minute from 10.10 a.m. to 10.30 a.m. on the monthly expiry day. This is intended to give an average figure which is difficult to manipulate and which may thus be relied upon.

However, the futures market is dominated by market-makers. And they are well aware of their opportunity and sometimes their compelling requirement to hold the market up or force it down in the run-up to and during the final twenty minutes of trading which determine the make-up figure. It may be wondered how they can do this. Quite simply, one firm might have an exposure of £1 million a FT-SE 100 point. A 25 point movement will cost £25 million. It pays mightily for it to bid up for stock or offer stock in FT-SE 100 constituents in the twenty minutes – depending upon which way its book is suited. Because the trade in the underlying constituents in the FT-SE 100 (as has been noted above) is frequently so thin, it is quite possible to affect the underlying FT-SE 100 average without incurring substantial losses when squaring the positions taken between 10.10 a.m. and 10.30 a.m.

For, although market-makers in FT-SE 100 constituents are obliged to deal at the prices shown on their screens and in certain minimum sizes, it will be found that, during the final minutes to the settlement of the make-up of the FT-SE 100, the market-making firm that is engaged in manipulation is curiously reluctant to answer its telephones. Of course, as soon as 10.30 a.m. has come and gone, they are open to all and sundry.

One reason why I advise the typical equities trader not to trade the

FT-SE 100 is that the best FT-SE 100 trader of whom I am aware never trades equities. This is because he has decided that he can trade one or the other but not both. In his opinion, the concentration required in respect of one sector of the market precludes concentrating on the other. He has chosen the FT-SE 100 and he spends something like £50,000 p.a. on information services alone. He holidays for a quarter of the year. But, when trading, he never leaves his desk except to answer the call of nature – and even when thus ensconced he is surrounded by telephones. Unless you are prepared to be as dedicated as that, you should think very carefully about trading the FT-SE 100 with a view to profit as a trader rather than merely insuring your portfolio.

FT-SE 250

Another stockmarket index (there is also a FT-SE 350 index) traded in London is the FT-SE 250 index, which is based on the next 250 companies in size after the first 100. It was developed in recognition that these companies frequently show a remarkably different average performance from that of the first 100. It might be thought that it is a tool to hedge either short or long positions in the underlying constituents. But the reality is that it is not yet a popular or well understood contract.

Trading in the FT-SE 250 is frequently thin. For instance, one might be minded to buy the FT-SE 250 against a short-sale of the FT-SE 100 (a form of straddle). But the reality is that any trade in the FT-SE 100 based on such a view would have to await the opening of a position in the FT-SE 250 so as to avoid a mismatch in sizes.

* * *

◆

CHAPTER EIGHT

CONTRACT FOR DIFFERENCES

◆

Borrowing stock; stamp duty; "contract for differences"; "Integrated Securities Houses"

An investor with an inquisitive turn of mind will reflect that it would be very helpful to borrow stock from time to time. This avoids closing when he might be otherwise compelled. However, he will find that a pure agency broker not only will not, but cannot borrow stock. This is because it has no licence to do so. But market-makers have – they need to be able to do so to allow short positions. And, where market-makers form part of an "integrated securities house" (henceforth ISH and so-called because the "house" integrates market-making, agency broking, corporate financial advisory services and so on), the ISH can borrow for its agency broking clients. This allows the ISH agency broker client to choose not to be bought-in. However, for such a facility to be available, the investor must be of substance and generating, other things being equal, in excess of £100,000 commission a year.

It is an immensely beneficial facility. Since it is not available to the client of a conventional agency broker (the traditional avenue of the private client) he may indeed be irritated by the fact that, when "renewing and cashing", he is constantly debited with 0.5% stamp duty whereas the opposition dealers are not. Avoidance of stamp duty cost is a very significant economy particularly when allied to avoidance of brokerage and the market-maker's turn on "renewing and cashing" – not to mention the interest credited or to be taken into account through release of funds to the investor who has borrowed stock – this is a possibility on the short tack and considered in greater detail below.

After all, say one were to hold a short position open for a year in the normal manner, one would probably have to "renew and cash" at least six times. On each occasion, one would have to pay brokerage, stamp duty and, from time to time, a small turn to the market-maker. These total perhaps 1.5% on each occasion or 9% in a year. It will be readily seen that no serious "hedge fund" (that is to say a fund which seeks from time to time to deploy short positions as policy in contrast to long positions) can decline stamp duty avoidance facilities when trading UK equities.

But it is more significant than that. When the ISH agency broker opens a short position for its client, it provides not a sale contract but the equivalent thereof as a contract note in respect of a "contract for differences". When the ISH agency broker buys to close on behalf of its client, no stamp duty is incurred. If one saves stamp duty (say) six times a year, one is talking money. If one cuts out the market-maker's turn and brokerage on each renewal, one can start booking tickets to the Bahamas. One can even stay there.

The "contract for differences" simply leads to a debit or credit to the client's statement when the purchase to close has been completed. I cannot think why going long should produce the same stamp duty-free result – but it does. In fact, I understand that the ISH agency broker will even consider dealing "net" (ie. no commission) just so that it can (discreetly) favour its own market-makers and attract sale instructions which release cash from the market which in turn yields interest to the ISH. For some reason, the ISH agency broker client does not get this interest (unless his account is very substantial) – he is merely debited with an "administration" fee in respect of the service that is the provision of stock. I suspect that the reason that this is so and that no or little interest is credited, is that there is little or no competition to provide such a financial service.

It should also be noted that "net" terms can be offered because market-making business is so profitable for the ISH that brokerage starts to be irrelevant.

Further, contracts for differences involve different disclosure rules as regards business done in the market and when. And there is no requirement to disclose a stake that would otherwise be discloseable under the Companies Act 1985 – this was highlighted early in 1995 when Trafalgar House, with the assistance of Swiss Banking Corporation, bid for Northern Electricity.

In the US, an agency client can borrow stock. But he has to return it the moment it is demanded back. That does not strike me as absurd because, presumably, if the ultimate beneficial owner wants it, he has sold it or will sell it and, therefore, the original short-seller is not being "squeezed". That said, it would be extremely irritating to deal with lenders who were to keep on demanding stock back. Presumably one can always return stock to a lender without notice. The lender does not necessarily know that one is short.

Which brings me to my next point: stock borrowing is surely straightforward with (say) a major FT-SE 100 constituent. The ISH is bound to have many clients with ISH nominee-registered holdings. Getting hold of the stock would be simplicity itself. And, if there were insufficient stock, a quick call to the market-making arm to go on the bid would suffice. But seeking to borrow the smaller stock could easily lead to trouble.

Another factor to take into account is that an agency broker acts for its client and does not tell anybody else that it has gone short. ISHs are in a different position. They claim that they maintain "Chinese walls" (the Chinese are taken to be inscrutable and impenetrable). But I do not believe in Chinese walls – I have always thought that (I can't resist it) they are a load of walls. And it just occurs to me that going round borrowing stock in a thinly traded stock could cause garrulity to break out. That would be bad news. And bad news travels fast, particularly where revenge is in point. Short-sellers attract jealousy and revenge.

If one asks a member of the staff of an ISH what their declared position is on all this, one gets a slightly coy response. The ISH knows that it enjoys a benefit improperly conducted (because there is inadequate competition) at the expense of its clients. It knows that this benefit avoids stamp duty – whereas the clients of pure agency brokers have to pay up. It knows that its trading advantage is a direct breach of the general principle of a "level playing field". As a result, the ISH staff member is discreet to the point of being downright uninformative. One should just persist.

* * *

◆

CHAPTER NINE

BEAR-RAIDING

◆

Definition of bear-raiding: S47 and defamation

There is some confusion over the meaning of the term "bear-raid". Simply selling a stock short does not constitute initiating or participating in a bear-raid. Bear-raiding occurs when the short–seller, having sold first, persuades others to sell after him so that the price goes down sufficiently to secure a profit for the first seller. The means of persuasion are varied. For those who are indifferent to lying, a simple lie to another dealer with whom one wishes to get even or merely "rot up" can work. But a story in the press takes more effort and should be more effective.

As it happens, I lie much less often than other people in general (although, for an intriguing study of the subject, I recommend that you read

The Penguin Book Of Lies edited by Philip Kerr). It also seems to me that lying is an inherent part of the human condition. This creates difficulties at the margin for people who are unable to be philosophical or who do not know their place. But whether all the foregoing is so or not, one point is certain: the law now precludes misleading statements and practices in relation to the stockmarket. This is regulated by S47 of the Financial Services Act 1986. As recounted elsewhere it can lead to a prosecution.

Another problem that can arise (although I have no personal experience of it) is to be on the receiving end of a writ for defamation. Although it is commonly supposed that only people can be defamed whereas companies cannot because companies do not have feelings, companies have legitimate commercial interests. To spread the rumour that Squeaky Clean PLC is questionable when, in fact, it is squeaky clean, is not merely unfair, it is actionable. Even if the plaintiff has no merit, a foolish bear-raider can face substantial legal expenses.

Fraud and fraudsters

Fraud is more widespread than one might at first suppose. It is practised by many allegedly respectable people – perhaps clearing bankers, for instance. For, as is well known, depositors at UK clearing banks could never withdraw all their savings if they were all to choose to withdraw them at the same time. Of course, this is a most unlikely embarrassment for the Government of the day because depositors with UK clearing banks are most unlikely so to behave. But it can be reasonably argued that the majority of depositors are the victim of a confidence trick. They have been "conned" into depositing their cash in the belief that they can have it back at any time they choose. Society tolerates this state of affairs because it reckons that it can live with it.

Well! Are clearing bankers alone in this behaviour? Most certainly not! For instance, I might be invited to lunch and telephone my host with the advice "I'll see you at Wiltons at one o'clock sharp". What I really mean is "I'll see you at Wiltons at one o'clock provided I do not have a heart attack on the way there". But, if one were to qualify all such acceptances in this manner, one would expend a disproportionate amount of time to no effect. Time does not permit the expression of truth. Society accepts this.

Confidence is vital in any commercial operation. He who cannot muster it need not bother to commence trading. It is really an expression of "I'm me. Trust me". All reasonable people recognise the wisdom of that presentation by a trader. After all, even if one has never traded oneself, one has many times attended the theatre and been transported by acting. One has seen something achieved.

Criminal law penalises deception where on balance another could be or has been hurt. And there is the problem: how does one determine the balance? After all, as we have seen, nearly all takers of credit in commerce deceive. The real question is the degree to which they have so behaved: has their behaviour been reasonable in relation to those who have extended credit?

And, actually (as you may be relieved to learn) most do not find this a difficult problem in practice. However, there are some who do. Leaving aside those who are tempted to desperate actions in the terminal period of a business, there are people who are born or moulded in childhood to deceive or consumed with the need to take revenge upon their fellow citizens through deceit.

It is partly that it saves quite a lot of hard work. After all, what could be simpler than advising the customer that the work has been done (when it has not and where the customer may take some years to find out the truth) and then rendering an invoice for settlement? And then there is the derivation of pleasure: there is no doubt to my mind that a principal motivation to deceive is the pleasure derived for the deceiver.

I have known an entrepreneur and his accountant operate for five years some twenty bank accounts (all at different branches of some five or so banks and in respect of twenty companies) cross-firing cheques simply to borrow about £100,000 in total against uncleared effects. As those of you who have not previously contemplated such conduct can appreciate, it entails an hour or so a day to work out and check each balance and frequent use of couriers to meet deadlines. The process has to continue every single business day of the year. It means that there is no such thing as a holiday. It entails massive bank charges. It entails drawing sudden short-term loans from (say) pawnbrokers to satisfy any bank employee who has come to wonder about the account. It is truly an engagement with hell. The only possible result is ultimate impoverishment. And the only possible motivation to persist with it (I am convinced that the fraudster had several opportunities to wind up the scheme) was a pleasure derived from it.

Is there any sure way of detecting a fraudster if one is merely an observer of an entrepreneur and his company? I doubt it. There are merely pointers. But a way to initiate the process of review is to consider whether you can ever get a straight answer to a straight question. In my experience, fraudsters have a unique ability to change the subject. They may bully the questioner or they may charm him. It does not matter how the questioner is deflected. The fact that deflection is practised is the important point.

A really competent fraudster devises a grand lie to support his act. This lie is so monstrous that it is accepted. Maxwell devised his "charitable" foundation, hidden in Liechtenstein, to control his commercial interests. Had he merely had a family investment holding company, resident and operated in the UK, many of his transactions would have been seen for what they were. But, by putting them offshore and giving them the cloak of some higher purpose beyond mere commerce, they came to be accepted. After all, not merely could he claim to be working for charity, he could show modesty by deferring to trustees. Of course, the audience was never in a position to check the claims. They went unchecked.

Another fraud is to devise a special fervour which is peculiar to the fraudster's company. For instance, about twenty-five years ago, an office equipment company (whose name I forget) established quite a stockmarket reputation because its staff never used Christian names but addressed one another as Mr Brown or Miss Smith or whatever. This manner of conduct was put about as evidence of high formality and moral rectitude. Actually, it was a cover for massive deception – the casual enquirer would typically learn nothing. Put another way, it meant that any outsider dealing with the staff found some special performance laid on which precluded the reasonable person's understanding of the staff and the company.

The general conclusion on the long tack is that one should beware of investing in any company that one does not understand. An extremely successful dealer whom I have known for many years always declines to invest in electronic companies because he does not understand electronics. Not even IBM is sufficiently large and seemingly endowed with momentum to tempt him to reconsider his stance. In short, he consciously declines to run the risk of being conned.

For the short-seller, the message is clear: as soon as a company is inexplicable, doubt it and put it on the short list. In the majority of cases, you will get a trading opportunity. Of course, you may have to wait some years because top class fraudsters have an astonishing tenacity to maintain the deception.

Insider trading

This book does not offer the opportunity to consider the present law in relation to insider trading. Suffice it to remark that the Government has so hopelessly misunderstood this subject (and over many years) that the chances of common sense being brought to bear are negligible in the foreseeable future. However, clearly, anybody who deals in shares without inside information (in the sense of information not generally appreciated by the market) is, as a French market speculator of late Victorian vintage once remarked, as stupid as he who buys cattle by moonlight. Further, I am attracted to the reform that it should be obligatory to deal only when in possession in fact or by claim of inside information. It would save so much trouble – not least the marketing of hypocrisy by fools, this time posing as regulators, pompously hectoring and deceiving a weary world.

But the short-seller is a frequent trader and since his style of trading will eventually throw up a major gain (in absolute or percentage terms) he can be caught by the law. And the way things are going, somebody is bound to be fingered when entirely innocent. The unswerving advice here offered is to say absolutely nothing to anybody. Regulators are sometimes people who have failed in their business or in life in general (because, if one stops for two seconds to think about it, it is obvious that nobody would choose to be a eunuch if he could also be the proprietor of the harem). As a result of their inferiority, they seek to pester others so that they can seem important.

Further, the law actively encourages and empowers them so to behave. So discretion is your friend. What may strike you as a chance and irrelevant reflection upon the success of a trade can be taken as potentially incriminating either directly by a regulator or through the agency of betrayal by someone whose livelihood is determined by a regulator. The eventual upshot may well be your acquittal. But the cost is worry and delay. However much you may hold the insider trading law in contempt, the power rests with those who implement it and you challenge that at your peril. With a bit of luck, this state of affairs should not continue forever. At least, I hope not. I also reckon that telephone-tapping by Government is on the way as an officially if clandestinely condoned means of reviewing traders' conduct. So watch your mouth. And, as for your pen, confine it to love letters and history in the public domain. Although England used to be an agreeable country in which to live, simply yearning for a return to carefree days will not bring them back.

* * *

Financial Services Act 1986

CHAPTER V

CONDUCT OF INVESTMENT BUSINESS

Misleading statements and practices.

47.—(1) Any person who—

(*a*) makes a statement, promise or forecast which he knows to be misleading, false or deceptive or dishonestly conceals any material facts; or

(*b*) recklessly makes (dishonestly or otherwise) a statement, promise or forecast which is misleading, false or deceptive,

is guilty of an offence if he makes the statement, promise or forecast or conceals the facts for the purpose of inducing, or is reckless as to whether it may induce, another person (whether or not the person to whom the statement, promise or forecast is made or from whom the facts are concealed) to enter or offer to enter into, or to refrain from entering or offering to enter into, an investment agreement or to exercise, or refrain from exercising, any rights conferred by an investment.

(2) Any person who does any act or engages in any course of conduct which creates a false or misleading impression as to the market in or the price or value of any investments is guilty of an offence if he does so for the purpose of creating that impression and of thereby inducing another person to acquire, dispose of, subscribe for or underwrite those investments or to refrain from doing so or to exercise, or refrain from exercising, any rights conferred by those investments.

(3) In proceedings brought against any person for an offence under subsection (2) above it shall be a defence for him to prove that he reasonably believed that his act or conduct would not create an impression that was false or misleading as to the matters mentioned in that subsection.

(4) Subsection (1) above does not apply unless—

(*a*) the statement, promise or forecast is made in or from, or the facts are concealed in or from, the United Kingdom;

(*b*) the person on whom the inducement is intended to or may have effect is in the United Kingdom; or

(*c*) the agreement is or would be entered into or the rights are or would be exercised in the United Kingdom.

(5) Subsection (2) above does not apply unless—

(*a*) the act is done or the course of conduct is engaged in in the United Kingdom; or

(*b*) the false or misleading impression is created there.

(6) A person guilty of an offence under this section shall be liable—

(*a*) on conviction on indictment, to imprisonment for a term not exceeding seven years or to a fine or to both;

(*b*) on summary conviction, to imprisonment for a term not exceeding six months or to a fine not exceeding the statutory maximum or to both.

Financial Services Act 1986. Section 47. "Misleading statements and practices."

CHAPTER TEN

THE THOUGHTS OF EVIL KNIEVIL

Capital and markets: a personal plea

When this book was being finalised, the publisher mentioned that I should take the opportunity to make any general observations in relation to markets that I felt worth making. He remarked that, since a platform had been established, it would be foolish not to use it.

And I start with the reminder that in the long run we are all dead. So, should we feel tempted to be contemptuous towards our governors, either political or imposed by statute, on the grounds that they have only thoughts for the short-term, we are obliged to reflect that, if civil peace is maintained and the country keeps going for a few more years, we have probably got off very lightly. Thus seeming indifference on the part of our governors to a particular political principle is made tolerable by another and overriding principle that whatever gives rise to peace has much to be said for it. Put another way, given that democracy is the best system of determining a Government we are ever likely to have, it is rather silly to rail against what it produces.

But the truth is that allowing politicians casually to advance their careers without comment can be immensely wasteful and destructive. And the problem becomes more pressing when the ground covered by politicians is complicated and way beyond the understanding of the general citizen in whose name legislation is passed.

Regulation of the securities industry

Accordingly, I now make the general proposition that the cause of wider share ownership has been the unconscious parent of a disastrous regulatory regime for the securities industry. It has also led to debilitating distortions in capital markets.

The fact is that regulation of the securities industry is now massively expensive and paid for by investors. It is probable that each year the costs of regulation now far exceed any conceivable loss through fraud. This is insane. Further, there is clear evidence that if any one individual within the industry stands up to criticise, he or she will immediately attract a flurry of clandestine activity to undermine their position. This is partly because regulators are the people they are – lightweights in the very industry they are seeking to regulate and thus minded to throw their weight around to compensate for their own inadequacies. And it is partly because they are so well paid that they have a massive vested interest in silly and presumptuous rules. Finally, because they are statutorily imposed, there is no way of getting rid of the regulators. They are just a permanent drain on resources.

That is not all. The regulators make up many of the rules as they go. As an example from the early days of the development of more detailed statute-based securities industry regulations in the UK, take the first South African approach by Anglo American upon Consolidated Goldfields in the early 1980s. The then chairman of the Takeover Panel commented that there should be more open disclosure of share stakes to inhibit the likes of Anglo American (then quite legitimately) building up an undisclosed shareholding in a British company through the jobbing system. Further, he felt that it would be unfair on a granny in Cornwall who could not assess what was happening to her shares in a "great British company". My mind boggled. First, as should have been obvious to even the most casual follower of the LSE, if ever a company could reasonably have been described as South African, Consolidated Goldfields was that company. Anglo American was simply seeking to acquire a South African industrial concern. The notion that Consolidated Goldfields was British, excepting in the sense that Britons dominated the register of shareholders, was emotive rubbish. Further, if it was the case that at the price proposed Consolidated Goldfields would depart to the South Africans for too low a value, one is bound to ask why such a transfer could ever have been contemplated. Finally, the notion of assisting thc granny in Cornwall supposes that she can be assisted in this manner. And, clearly, she cannot.

Again, I suppose that it must be attractive to politicians to feel able to claim that they have "cleaned up" the "City". And, if they felt that they had even half a chance, I expect that they would claim that they have cancelled adultery. They are certainly sufficiently stupid to try it on.

But no amount of "cleaning up" the "City" can obscure the truths that in the long run brokers and market-makers profit from a stock exchange and that a few investors consistently make above average returns while the vast majority of investors achieve indifferent or worse results. I stress the long run because it depends on what one means by the short run. As I remarked earlier in the section on "normal" markets, investors in equities have done fairly well since 1919. And, as Harold Wilson did not remark, 76 years is a long time in politics.

However, I still think that we should seek to discern the long view and assert that it must always be wise to look for eternal truths. And one of them is that we should avoid needless costs. The background to the development and toleration of these costs is perhaps less obvious.

Starting with the virtually unregulated days, in the section on short-sellers of the past and, in particular, Vanderbilt and three corners, I touched upon the astonishing conduct of the commercial America of his time. I sometimes wish that we might return to such a society and its absence of regulation. For a start, there would be no regulators to pay. However, the truth is that such a regime would entail wholesale corruption and abuses of power. And these would not be desirable even if, as a libertarian, I always seek to reserve the right to let others decide for themselves as to how they wish to behave.

Of course, once we have decided to accept some regulation, we are thereafter discussing degree. And, yet, quite frequently, in recent years, when contemplating the drafting of statute-based regulation of the securities markets, the common sense tests of illegality of behaviour and remedies in relation thereto have always been available but ignored. For instance, legislation relating to prospectuses renders it an offence to make a misleading statement. But any investor who relies upon such a statement has always had a common law right to sue for damages arising from such a statement and where he can prove he or she has suffered loss as a result of the misleading statement.

Investor protection legislation

What is even more deplorable about the current law and requirements for stockmarket listing is that the expenses of achieving a listing are frequently a significant amount of the net assets floated. And there is no way of avoiding this. What should occur with each flotation is that the prospective investor should have his own checklist of information required (and the degree of certification to be provided) and then decide for himself.

Further, and as recent years have shown, despite the expensive investor protection legislation currently in force and relating to flotations, an appreciable number of flotations have proved to be very disappointing within a short period. This was because the market was prepared to overlook important reasons for holding back from taking up the stock. That was the condition of markets. The effect of these failures has been to damage the credibility of the issuing houses concerned. That seems to me to be quite as important a sanction as any programme of legislation. It is much more readily understood by all and it is much cheaper and more flexible.

Nor indeed is there evidence that the prospectus rules are capable of being anything like sufficiently flexible. I write here from personal experience: In 1987, I became executive chairman of a company that was in deep trouble, Winebank PLC, which had been ravaged by my predecessor, a fraudster. When I first inspected the books of the company the liability position was not clear. Nothing daunted, I set about suing the fraudster to recover funds that he had misappropriated – in this I was not successful. On the other hand, the criminal prosecution succeeded and the fraudster received a custodial sentence and was disqualified as a director. In that sense, my chairmanship was wholly successful because I am certain that had I put the company into liquidation as soon as I had doubted its insolvency the creditors would have got less and the fraudster would have got clean away.

Unfortunately, Winebank itself went into compulsory liquidation on the petition of HM Customs and Excise because I could not economically raise fresh capital. I had foreseen that this difficulty would arise but was completely hamstrung in raising the capital by the prospectus rules where the cost of their application would inevitably have proved grossly disproportionate to any benefit that might accrue to the company. So, far from the prospectus rules assisting the process of raising capital, they actively contributed to its dereliction.

Insider trading

Similarly, the objection to insider trading (as defined by the legislation) is not that it is a breach of the legislation. It is that it is offensive to steal other people's information or to use information from other people knowing that it has been improperly acquired either from them or by them. I would much sooner that the thrust of prosecution had started at that point and considered theft or breach of trust – two causes of action and prosecution that have been available under our law long before any member of the Cabinet had been born. If it were argued that evidential difficulties would be considerable on this basis, I would remark that there is little evidence that they would be any more considerable than those encountered under the insider trading legislation that we have today.

Nor are these difficulties confined to the Conservative party, which promulgated the insider trading legislation. It is frequently argued by those on the left of politics that the stockmarket is a casino whose fluctuations damage the lives of ordinary people. The immediate riposte to such a claim is that whatever else the stockmarket is or is not, it is not a casino. For a casino gives results that in the long run always favour the owner of the casino and are, to the extent that the gambler is favoured, based on pure luck rather than good judgement. Were it a casino, there would be a point to ponder: after all, why should the majority of citizens have their lives materially affected and possibly diminished by random-result-tolerating gamblers? But, since that is not the position, the only point to consider is the effect of fluctuations.

Some argue that excessive fluctuations in individual share prices or markets in general are unsettling to the economy. But those are hard to foresee (and to judge a fluctuation as excessive it must be capable of being seen so in advance of the correcting movement). I know that this is so because I have often tried to foresee the excess myself so as to profit by the correcting movement! As to the degree to which they are unsettling, I suppose it depends on how people react to fluctuations. If you are naturally given to panicking then I suppose that some fluctuation may not be ideal for you. But, for most, it does no harm to cause people to contemplate the uncertain nature of life. Indeed, it probably does quite a lot of good.

I suppose that if fluctuations are wild (but by what measure) they may tend to cause investors or as those engaged in a commercial concern to be less confident in their handling of their affairs. If so, wild fluctuations are to be avoided. But a sensible and reasonable person confronted by this difficulty simply reduces his exposure for all time or perhaps steers clear of exposure at the outset. And if it were argued that his customer's confidence and equilibrium might not be as readily maintained in the face of fluctuating markets, I would reply that his customer will just have to learn to brace up. It is not as though he is being asked to toughen the sinews of war.

In any event, from time to time, confidence generally arises in or departs from the economy even though it always returns to the normal level provided by the human condition – which I presume to be unaltered taking one century with another. It is affected by wars, technological improvement, disease or migration – to name but a few factors. It just is not possible artificially to stimulate maintained confidence or persistently to depress confidence. Interestingly, this very point was, I think, made by a past Chancellor of the Exchequer, Lord Lawson, who remarked that booms come and go and that they are beyond the scope of Governments to control. If he is right (and I am pretty sure he is), then all discussion of the advantages of the control of fluctuations is seriously diminished in scope.

The idea behind determining by statute-based regulation those who can handle investments and those who cannot may give a temporary climate in which investors are less frequently deceived or misled or, worse, deprived of all or part of their savings. But, in the long run, surely, the responsibility for selecting advisers or agents must be left with individuals dealing with one another on a person to person basis. Life just cannot permit any automatic assumption of probity beyond that offered by individuals as such or in trade association.

The coming disaster

For instance (and here I do not wish to be considered a lord of misrule) my bet is that the new and profoundly impersonal central stock registration system currently being finalised by the Bank of England, upon which so many will rely, will give rise to a massive fraud. This will be because people will become complacent and presume that all is well. When the fraud occurs (2020AD?) the bemusement will be wondrous to behold. I will probably be dead by then. However, triumphantly, from the grave, I shall moan, as only a ghost can, into the ears of my grandchildren that they ought never to have spent the money on impersonal administration and regulation. I think that they will agree. But it will be too late for society to recover the preceding fifty years' failure to recognise the centrality of individual relationships and responsibility.

In any review of the place of stockmarkets in society, it is not possible to presume that investors can expect to be rewarded simply by their propensity to save. The fact is that if they are seen by others, who are less able and less well off, to be getting more than their fair share of the general wealth, there will always be popular resentment. In turn, this will always produce an economic climate in which profits appear uncertain. For profits above and beyond a living wage rely upon consent from the bulk of the members of society.

> ***"It is not possible for any Government economically to legislate for the man in the street to enjoy a permanent and successful engagement in the capital markets."***

This makes me doubt whether the constant stimuli to saving, promoted by the Government, can have any chance of producing an economic or politically desirable result in the long run. The scope for stimuli just runs out of road. (I think that there is an argument for a Government consciously to persuade children to save. But you will be relieved to learn that I do not here propose to consider the nation's youth education programme. Besides, I presume that my polemic considers adults alone).

There have been many examples of these misplaced stimuli. One of them, the inconsistent treatment of taxation of savings instruments has really been part of the Government's development of "popular capitalism" (an absurd misrepresentation of possibility) and allegedly based on the idea that most people can or should participate in the management and deployment of capital. But most people cannot do so beyond engaging in the consumption of the products and the application of capital. To pretend otherwise is basically deceitful.

The meddling (and I think that the venture capital promotion legislation offers a good example) has time and again proved fruitless. It has never been cheap to apply and it has caused wealthy individuals to presume absurdly excessive rates of return on capital as of right. Once weaned on such greed, it is very hard to persuade such investors to make a modest and reasonable claim that can be entertained by society in general.

For the same reasons, proffering a stream of sure-fire stagging profits on privatisation issues must be equally counterproductive. For what can be supplied once the stock of possible privatisations runs out?

Final thoughts

As another example of Governmental failure to handle capital markets, one need only take the issue of Personal Equity Plans. Here, fiscal inconsistency, distortion of capital markets, misadministration and hypocrisy are fused with liberal political deceit in attendance. There is no conceivable reason why such plans should be exempted from income and capital gains taxes given that these two taxes are generally applied within the economy. But these plans have been pushed as a means of buying votes (the assuaging of the middle classes). Indeed, they have now been pushed so far that yield bases to allow comparison of different applications of capital are profoundly unsatisfactory. The expense to the saver/investor of these developments is typically 1% p.a. and more of the capital invested. Had any previous Government proposed that 1% of the capital of all investors' money invested in a particular manner be wasted annually on form-filling solely caused by regulation and protection of title, it would have been laughed out of existence.

While comment upon Governmental folly in these areas of taxation and administration is not strictly speaking part of an argument against its judgement in relation to regulation of the securities industry, it is relevant in the sense that these errors in policy render a mature and sober approach to capital markets on the part of society in general much harder to attain.

All this muddle has been caused by seeking to attain the unattainable. For it is not possible for any Government economically to legislate for the man in the street to enjoy a permanent and successful engagement in the capital markets. He should be left alone, unprotected and with no guarantees and just as his grandparents taught him: modest, sceptical and reserved. Other things being equal, he should confine himself to FT-SE 100 stocks, preferably held in collective and managed investment schemes.

* * *

◆

APPENDIX ONE

SHORT-SELLING: THE LONDON STOCK EXCHANGE POSITION

◆

In September 1994, the London Stock Exchange issued a *consultation document* titled

Regulation of short-selling of UK equities and related securities during secondary offers

The subject of secondary offers is outside the scope of this book but the following are extracts which relate to the practice of short-selling:

Selling Practices – 'the principal issue'

- The Exchange does not consider that in most instances short-selling has a harmful effect on the market. It appears to be a valid and important part of the market making process and enables market makers to provide continuous, firm, two-way prices at times when they might not have stock on their books.

- Moreover, in normal market conditions in which neither the potential buyers nor sellers are being influenced unduly by the terms under which an offer of further shares in a company is being made, it remains a legitimate way in which to take a position in the company's securities. In these circumstances, any fall in the price resulting from selling activity will eventually be met by buying demand when investors consider that the price no longer adequately reflects a fair price for the company's shares.

Regulation of sales in the United States

The US takes a robust line in regulating short-selling.

- The scope for manipulation during offers is restricted under rule 10b-21, the Securities Exchange Act of 1934, by prohibiting all short-sellers in the lead up to an offer from covering their sales with the shares being offered. The rule does not restrict sales from inventory.

- The practice of short-selling of exchange listed securities is constrained by SEC rule 10a-1 which allows short-sales only where they have been carried out on an 'up-tick'; that is, where the short-sale occurs at a price that is above the last, previous trade in the security.

- The NASD which operates NASDAQ, a screen based competing market-maker system, has an analogous up-tick rule, that requires short sales to be traded above the best available displayed bid (the inside bid) or at the inside bid if the previous inside bid was lower. These rules are intended to reduce market volatility and counteract potential market manipulation. Arrangements are also in place for the publication of the aggregate short positions for securities listed on the principal exchanges on a monthly basis.

Short-selling practices in other markets

Australia

Short-selling of certain approved securities is allowed subject to the following restrictions:

- total short-sales in any approved security may not represent in excess of 10% of that approved security.
- a client must advise his broker when placing a short-selling order
- a 20% margin is required
- short-sales may not be made in a falling market or during a takeover offer
- any short-sale must be settled not later than 10 days after trade.

Austria

Short-selling is not banned in Austria. However, the central settlement system has the right to demand buy-in if settlement of transactions is delayed by lack of delivery and there are no stock borrowing facilities, making short-selling impractical.

Germany

Short-selling is not officially permitted although some 'informal' arrangements are made.

Hong Kong

The laws and taxation on short-selling are currently being relaxed in Hong Kong to facilitate the development of a derivatives market. Short-selling is permitted both by market-makers and clients but a margin of 125% is required to cover borrowing costs and covering. It is therefore expensive. Hitherto stock borrowing has been possible but has attracted stamp duty and constituted a disposal for tax purposes.

France

Short-selling is permitted and as in the UK there are few rules. Stock borrowing is common, except that a broker cannot close a short position using stock he is holding as a custodian.

Singapore

No short-selling in Singapore.

South Africa

A brief review of the rules of the JSE suggests that the buyer has a right to demand stock buy-in for delivery. It is therefore unlikely that short-selling is widespread in practice.

South Korea

Short-selling has been reintroduced after a period of prohibition in order to provide liquidity in the market. There are no formal market-makers but local investment banks often have proprietary holdings which they can lend to private clients. This is not a common feature.

Taiwan

Short-selling is permitted for domestic investors only and is limited to $600,000 per account.

Japan

Short-selling, other than when undertaken following the borrowing (including delivery) of stock prior to the time of trade, is not permitted. The Tokyo Exchange works on four-day rolling settlement which imposes a further barrier against fulfilling a short position.

◆

APPENDIX TWO

RECOMMENDED READING

◆

Rushmere Wynne Limited

Rushmere Wynne specialises in the publication of books for the private investor. Its current list includes the following titles;

THE PROSHARE GUIDE TO YOU AND YOUR STOCKBROKER

by John Cobb

(1993: Price £9.95 Paperback) ISBN 0–948035–03–X.

This book explains how to choose a stockbroker who can meet your own special needs.

THE INVESTORS' HANDBOOK

by Maggie Drummond

(1994: Price £6.95 Paperback) ISBN 0–948035–04–8.

An excellent introduction to the basics of stockmarket trading.

THE SECOND FINANCIAL SERVICES REVOLUTION

by Brian Tora

(1994: £12.95 Hardback) ISBN 0–948035–10–2.

For the investor who wants to understand what is happening in the revolution of the world of financial services, this book is a must.

THE PRIVATE INVESTOR'S GUIDE TO THE STOCKMARKET

by Neil Stapley

(1994: Price £8.95 Paperback) ISBN 0–948035–11–0.

One of the best introductions to the stockmarket yet written by a leading private client stockbroker. The book explains how to build your share portfolio, how to evaluate shares, how to assess risk and much much more.

HOW TO MAKE A KILLING IN THE ALTERNATIVE INVESTMENT MARKET

by Michael Walters

(1995: £9.95 Paperback) ISBN 0–948035–14–5.

The Deputy City Editor of the *Daily Mail,* Michael Walters, writes the third in his best selling trilogy of books for his numerous readers.

TRADED OPTIONS – A PRIVATE INVESTOR'S GUIDE:
how to invest more profitably
by Peter Temple
(1995: Price £16.95 Hardback) ISBN 0–948035–06–4
Written by the author and journalist, Peter Temple, the book explains traded options in a step-by-step style. It is sponsored by LIFFE and ProShare.

EVERY WOMAN'S GUIDE TO PERSONAL FINANCE
by Rosanna Spero
(1995: Price £9.99 Paperback) ISBN 0–948035–15–3
Daily Mail journalist Rosanna Spero provides a practical guide for women of all ages and stages in the management of their finances. Jeff Prestridge, Personal Finance Editor of the *Financial Mail on Sunday* describes it as "one of the best books I have read in a long time..."

INVESTMENT CLUBS:
The low-risk way to stockmarket profits
by Tony Drury
(1995: Price £6.99 Paperback) ISBN 0–948035–22–6
Would you like to become a successful stockmarket investor? You can, by reading this book. Experience the fun and fellowship of investing in a low-risk way, within the confines of an investment club.

HOW TO MAKE A KILLING IN PENNY SHARES
by Michael Walters
(1995: Price £9.99 Paperback) ISBN 0–948035–20–X
Already sold 50,000, this is the up-dated version of the best seller written by the Deputy City Editor of the *Daily Mail,* Michael Walters.

THE VISIONARY INVESTOR:
how to use a PC to make more profitable stockmarket decisions
by David Linton
(1995: Price £19.99 Hardback) ISBN 0–948035–16–1
A leading PC investment software expert advises on how to buy and set up a PC system and how to use the information to make better stockmarket decisions (includes the Internet).

CHARTERS ON CHARTING:
how to improve your stockmarket decision making.
by David Charters
(1995: £12.95 Hardback) ISBN 0–948035–21–8
Already on its third reprint, this book has become a classic. It explains how charting works. Described by *the Investors' book club* as "the best charting book for the private investor we have seen."

All these books are available from leading bookshops or by writing to:

Rushmere Wynne Limited:
Cavalier House, 21 High Street,
Leighton Buzzard, Beds. LU7 7DN.
Telephone: 01525 853726
Fax: 01525 852037.

Any reader purchasing any title is entitled to a 20% discount off the listed price. To obtain this just write to, or phone, Rushmere Wynne and mention this book.

INDEX